I'M FINE!

ENDA O'DOHERTY

WITH DERMOT KEYES

Social Media

www.endaodoherty.ie
YouTube: Enda O Doherty
Twitter: @GoEndaOdoherty
Facebook: Enda O Doherty Keynote Speaker
Facebook: The Mental Health Challenge

I'm Fine!

Thoughts on Life, Addiction, Love and Health

Enda O'Doherty

with *Dermot Keyes*

RED STRIPE PRESS

Published by
Red Stripe Press
an imprint of
Orpen Press
Upper Floor, Unit B3
Hume Centre
Hume Avenue
Park West Industrial Estate
Dublin 12
Ireland

email: info@orpenpress.com
www.orpenpress.com

Paperback ISBN 978-1-78605-105-9
ePub ISBN 978-1-78605-106-6

This book is designed to provide information and support to our readers. It is not intended as a substitute for professional advice from mental health professionals. The reader should always consult a relevant professional when required. The content of this book is the sole expression and opinion of the author. No warranties or guarantees are expressed or implied by the publisher's choice to include any of the content in this volume. Neither the publisher nor the author shall be liable for any physical, psychological, emotional, financial or commercial damages, including, but not limited to, special, incidental, consequential or other damages.

Printed in Dublin by SPRINTprint Ltd

Thank You

To my wife, Maeve, and children, Clodagh, Fionn, Oisín. Your love, kindness and support are the foundation on which my dreams have been built. Forever grateful to you.

To the two teams who walked, crawled, smiled, laughed through the two adventures. Your passion and endless effort, simply put, saved lives, Thank you.

To our sponsors, supporters, families and friends your time and effort makes you part of this adventure forever. My sincerest thanks.

This book is dedicated to those who have lost loved ones to suicide. It is dedicated to those whose hearts are broken or are struggling through the darkest of times. This book is dedicated to you. I hope it stands as a beacon of light. Just like you, I too was lost and struggling. There is always hope. Behind every storm cloud, I promise you, is beautiful sunshine. You just must fight like hell for your life; your dawn will come. Thank you for reading my story.

Belfast to Waterford team

Maeve O'Doherty, Clodagh O'Doherty, Liam Maher, Dáire Grant, Anne Sinnott, Mark Duffy, Margaret Molloy, Nicky Quinlan, Jamie Long, Benny Smith, Kate Hayes, Eoin Keane, Denise Doyle, James Connelly, Benny Smith

The Kilimanjaro Crew

Martin Freeman, Evelyn Lyons, Linda Coughlan, Cecily Johnston, James Wheelan, Judy Browne-Allen, Martin Molloy, Jenny Carlyle, Louise Leahy, Peter Shanahan, Anne Byrne, Dáire Grant, Eoghan Sweeney, Cáit Ní hÁilín, Aisling Powell, Ollie Giltenane, Lisa Walsh, Olive Ruane, Lauren Traynor, Leslie Cusack-Hughes, Enda O'Doherty, John Deegan, Tim O'Carroll, Denise Doyle, Eoin Keane, Jamie Roche, Eileen Acheson, Maeve O'Doherty, Jason DeCourcy, Louise Walsh, Gary Freeman

Foreword

Sadly, I had a personal experience of losing someone I love to suicide and the shock of this left me devastated. I went through a grief process that anyone who loses someone to suicide will experience but I felt I had to do something. I started reading everything I could on suicide and after a long time of reading and researching I knew that I had to find a way to be a voice that changes how society thinks about suicide and self-harm. So, with the support of my husband, we founded Pieta House.

I'm so delighted to be asked to write a foreword for this inspiring and unique book. Enda's message was clear and simple. He carried a washing machine to remind people not to carry a heavy load, to reach out to ask for help but equally importantly to remind each of us to be aware that people near us can often be struggling in secret and need our support.

I don't think I can ever forget the image of him walking into Dublin to meet me with his washing machine on his back surrounded by his supporters. His inspirational challenge of walking from Belfast to Waterford and later climbing Mount Kilimanjaro, with his washing machine, has inspired and been a beacon of hope for so many people.

The messages of hope, kindness, love, care and optimism resonate through every chapter of this wonderful book.

> *'If you are working on something that you really care about, you don't have to be pushed. The vision pulls you'* - *Steve Jobs.*

Reading this book, you will see that Enda's vision has pushed him to places most can't imagine being. As you read through this book, I hope you will be reminded of the Robert Siltanen quote:

> *'Those who are crazy enough to think they can change the world are very often the ones who do.'*

Joan Freeman
Founder of Pieta House, Senator 2016-2020

Contents

1

Adventurous Beginnings

'What is your vocation? To be a good person.'

Marcus Aurelius, *Meditations*

5 December 2014. I'm chatting with Maeve in a Waterford city café when she poses the question:

'What are you going to do next: Another Ironman?'

Enda: 'No. I mean, I'd love to do another Ironman – the only interest I'd have in doing a third one would be to qualify for [the World Championship in] Hawaii, but the only way I'm qualifying for Hawaii is with stomach-stapling surgery! I'm never going to get down to the body weight I need to drop to, to get the speed I need to sustain – and it'd be a pretty big chunk of change to enter and get all of ye out there with me. And I'd be putting in 12 to 14 hours of training a week to get there, so no, not another Ironman. But I think it's about time I did something for charity, you know, and raise a few bob while I'm doing it.'

Maeve: 'So what do you have in mind?'

Enda: 'Well, it's got to be something with a story to it and a bit of imagination. How about walking from Belfast to Waterford?'

Maeve: 'Is that all?'

Anyone in a long-term relationship is accustomed to the tone of a partner, and its many different frequencies, subtexts and complexities. And the lilt of Maeve's query as I floated my next big idea formed the kernel of the adventure which ultimately led me, a washing machine and a life-changing supporting cast to take on most of the eastern Irish seaboard for a big walk unlike any other. And all it took to light the nine marathons in eight days fuse was Maeve's three-word question-cum-rallying-cry.

Jokingly, I replied: 'Oh and I'm going to carry a washing machine all the way while I'm at it.'

Now the message attached to it, profound as it is, wasn't running through my mind there and then – that came later. But Maeve's question, and the manner in which she put it to me, brought the morning I woke up and told her that I was going to stop drinking back to mind. In reply, she had said: 'That's great. Are you?' But the way she said it had me convinced that she wasn't convinced. As far as I was concerned, her body language was bellowing: 'Not in a million years will you give it up, even if you really wanted to.'

Maeve had ample reason to feel that way. Ask anyone living with an addict about how impotent and empty words can be from the mouth of a substance abuser. But here I stand. Sober. And happy on it.

With the decision about the walk mentally made and locked in, I realised I was going to have to get the word out about it, and that's where Facebook came into my life. As someone born in 1968, Facebook pre-December 2014 amounted to a book leaning against my face as I dozed off. Mr Zuckerberg's creation was an alien entity in my life until the time came to start spreading what ultimately became the Pieta Challenge message. With no skills or knowledge of what Facebook entailed, I'd heard enough chatter about it to realise it could serve a purpose for me, and my first post came a day after Maeve's game-changing question, on 6 December 2014. It simply read: 'Belfast to Waterford Walk' and it generated a grand total of two 'likes' – one from Maeve, the other from my best friend, Ailbhe Conway. The post itself amassed four views, while six people shared it. Talk about small beginnings!

Now, I could have looked at those initial numbers and felt as useful as a chocolate teapot, but I'd already bought fully into my idea. I believed in what I was doing and I believed I was doing it for the right reasons. I can remember having a conversation with my brother and he put it to me: 'Enda, this is an awful thing to be taking on.' By then, the idea of fundraising for Pieta House in tandem with the walk had taken root, and I outlined how I could justify committing to such an effort:

'Look, ten people die by suicide in this country every week. You have kids. I have kids. By the time we have grandkids, what are you or I going to say if one of them asks: "Grandad, there were 10 people dying by suicide every week in Ireland back before I was born. Why were so many people marching about water charges while people were dying like that? Why weren't the grown-ups back then talking about the really important things, and why didn't anyone stand up and say, right, we've got to do something to try and stop this?"'

And that made what I felt compelled to do crystal clear.

Death by suicide in twenty-first-century Ireland is not the equivalent of, say, genocide in Nazi Germany or Rwanda. But people in both those countries and elsewhere during both those terrible traumas who could have done something to stem the tide of death either didn't do enough or opted to stay silent and do nothing. Millions paid lip service and went with the crowd, as hundreds of thousands of people were incinerated and macheted out of existence.

The crowd can be wrong. The road more frequently travelled is not the path we should necessarily take simply because it's easier and more convenient. John Wooden, the great UCLA basketball coach, was a great believer in the power of words and he was a great exponent of how best to use them.

Consider the following:

'Why is it that so many non-attainers are quick to criticise, question and belittle the attainers? Why is it so hard for us to understand that we cannot antagonise and positively influence at the same time? Why is it so much easier to complain about the things we do not have than to make the most of and appreciate the things we do have.'[1]

In that same vein, why do so many of us opt to sit on the sidelines, shrug our shoulders and conclude that, as an individual, one's thoughts, words and actions ultimately mean very little. According to whom? The imp on your shoulder? I'm asking all of these questions without losing sight of the fact that I, Enda O'Doherty, as an individual Irish citizen, am not going to revolutionise mental health services in this country. I may be strongly idealised and well-intentioned, but I am not naïve when it comes to my place in the food chain. I do know that when I put my head on the pillow each and every night, should a grandchild of mine, many years from now, asks me about those ten people a week, I'll be able to say, 'here's what I did, let me tell you about it. Let me tell you that I tried'. And I hope by the time that conversation may well come around, that if enough people in this generation have tried, then the next generation won't be standing at gravesides in the numbers that so many youngsters and parents have in Ireland over the past 20 years, full of grief, left with unanswered questions and an empty space at the dinner table.

So I took to the infant Facebook page and created a very simple poster composed of white text on a red background, titled 'The Pieta Challenge', and it took me an hour and a half to put that piece of hi-tech mastery together. It generated two likes: the first click was by Gillian Tyrrell, whom I used to play badminton with, the second from Kevin McGrath, an architect who ultimately offered help in building Pieta House in Waterford.

Why Pieta House? That's down to one remarkable woman named Joan Freeman; the woman who set the ball rolling, the woman who told herself that more had to be done to prevent death by suicide and in turn shared her story with her neighbourhood, her city and her country. Her vocation was one I wanted to support, something I wanted to tell my grandchildren about, many years from now. In 2006, determined to make an imprint in the treatment of people reporting suicidal ideation in this country, Joan put up the home she shares with her husband and four children as collateral so that she could borrow €130,000 from her bank. And with that money, she opened the first Pieta House in Lucan.

'My husband would be awake every night terrified but I never doubted for a second that it wouldn't work,' Joan said in an interview with *The Journal*. 'Within months, people started donating and fundraising. It was an extraordinary thing to watch.'

Within nine years of the Lucan Centre opening its doors, 20,000 people had been helped in nine different Pieta Houses across the country. Joan Freeman's inspiration and the power of her message was something I wanted to buy into. And I was determined to do my bit to raise the monies that would be required to establish a Pieta House in Waterford. It remains one of the best decisions I've ever made.

And why a washing machine? Well, I knew that a challenge of this kind required a gimmick. I knew I needed something that would not only elicit unprecedented physical demands of me, but would generate column inches, sound bites and airtime on TV and radio. I needed a literal load to carry, a visible illustration of the mental load that so many people in this country are burdened by on a daily basis, a state of mind that proves overwhelming for some, tragically. I wanted to let as many people as possible know that sharing the load can make life easier and that a relative, friend or colleague could benefit from simply asking them a very short but hugely significant question: how are you? Not only that, but if you're the overburdened one, reaching out, asking for help and sharing the load has the potential to make your life immeasurably better. For so much of my own time in the fog, I didn't share the load. I drank instead. Then the light got back in and the axis of my life tilted – for the better.

Back to 6 December 2014. Maeve and I were heading into town, and Maeve logically put it to me: 'You'd better go find some way of carrying this washing machine,' so I popped into Mc's Outdoor Store, a well-stocked shop on The Quay which had everything you could think of when it comes to hiking, mountaineering and so on. I was perusing through the store's range of boots, straps and harnesses when Owen Keane, a sales assistant there and a deep-voiced giant of a man, walked my way and asked if I required any help. Little did I know that a friendship was about to forged with the gentlest man I've ever met.

I told Owen about these straps I was looking for: to attach to a bag was how I initially put it. But it became apparent to both of us that I was hiding something; I was too embarrassed to tell him about what I wanted to carry in the bag I was seeking out straps for. Telling someone you intend to carry a washing machine is the moment security gets called, before being asked to leave the shop – at least that's how I imagined the scenario beforehand! So Owen logically asked: 'What are you hoping to put in the bag,' to which I eventually replied: 'I'm hoping to strap the bag to a washing machine, and my plan is to carry the washing machine from Belfast to Waterford and raise funds for Pieta House.' He picked out a bag and then said he'd track down a full harness – a backpack without the bag – from a company called Berghaus, and that he might be able to make it walk-ready for me. But in the middle of our conversation, he headed off for a chat with the store manager, Ronan McDonagh, and I honestly thought I might be lucky enough to get a free pair of socks, a handshake and a 'best of luck with the walk' greeting when Owen came back to me. Maybe they might even put out a collection box in the shop for me.

But back came Owen, and what he said almost left me needing a harness to remain vertical. 'Right,' he said, in full man-on-a-mission mode. 'That's sorted.' To which I replied: 'You mean, the harness?' To which Owen replied: 'No, I'm taking my holidays to go on the walk with you.' Our verbal, albeit entirely amiable, tennis match continued.

Enda: 'But you've only just met me. I don't know you. You don't know me.'

Owen: 'Yeah, but you seem like a really interesting fella, and you seem to be doing this for all the right reasons. Someone has to do something about this [the country's suicide rate]. And I'm in. I've had a chat there with Ronan and I've booked my summer holidays for next year so that I can go on the walk with you.'

I couldn't really take it in. I'd met this gentle giant of a man only minutes previously, yet here he was, my first recruit! We shook hands heartily and I met up with Maeve who asked me if I'd gotten boots for myself. 'No,' said I, 'the bag is in hand alright, and I've also got the first person signed up to come with us.' A mixture of delight and surprise – and perhaps relief since it now appeared that someone she wasn't married to had bought into her husband's mad idea – was etched all over Maeve's face. It was no longer just the wacky O'Dohertys taking to the road with only a heavy white appliance for company. There's three of us in this now – a team – a green shoot of a team granted, but nonetheless a team. And it felt good. Really, really good.

I was still firmly in the naïve stages of promoting the whole endeavour. I genuinely didn't have a clue what I was doing, but I slowly began to find my feet. The day after Owen signed up, I went back to the shop and posed for a photo with Ronan with the gear the shop had presented me with, and that snap got 67 'likes' on Facebook. Having graduated from just two 'likes' on my first post, this really felt like progress.

Maeve logically put it to me that for a walk like this, I was going to need to tap into some expert physical know-how, so I got in touch with a past pupil of mine, Conor McDonald. I met him at the gym and the initial interaction between us was bizarre: the only relationship we'd had prior to that was that I was Conor's teacher and he was my student. But within 10 seconds of our conversation beginning, there was no doubt that those roles had been reversed! He was lord and master and I would do what I was told when I was told, an odd experience for someone in a job like mine.

Conor has commanding knowledge of his brief. He told me about his hopes and dreams, along with his philosophy on physical training, which was totally different to anything I'd previously been exposed to. That first night, after just 20 minutes, my session with Conor was over. And I was dry. As someone who had competed in Ironman and triathlon events, being dry at the end of a session just didn't compute with me. And how could I have achieved any benefits on the basis of 20 minutes work, at low intensity? Precision exercise? To me, this felt crazy and I made for home that night thinking I'd made a mistake. But Conor and his team, including Geina McGrath, told me to trust the process - and they really took care of me. And through the Modified Strongman Programme they really taught me how to exercise.

Just like the Strongman events that we've all caught at least a glimpse of on television, where contestants take on the Farmer's Lift, carrying the yoke - the metal frame that you bear on your shoulders - pull-ups, dips, there was a lot of very limited, strict movements that Conor was looking for. And his plan was for me to train for five to six months with him and then for me to hit the road and start building up the miles with the washing machine. After that first night in the gym with Conor I posted a photo on my Facebook page with a very simple message - 'Thank You' - and we jumped up to 1,500 views. And I began to realise that people not only wanted hope, but they also wanted information and a dollop of entertainment thrown in for good measure! Quite soon after that, I posted my first training video and it was heavily viewed: we seem to love watching people putting themselves through physical exertion! But again, it was all helping to spread the word, and I was completely fine with that.

By mid-December 2014, the rolling stone was beginning to gather some serious moss, and my thoughts began to turn to plotting the route and schedule of the walk. I'd set my sights on eight days - I could have opted for 10 - but I felt we might only hold people's attention for so long. The plan was to do about 30 miles each day, taking in the following: Belfast–Banbridge, Banbridge–Dundalk, Dundalk–Drogheda, Drogheda–Dublin, Dublin–Newbridge, Newbridge–Carlow, Carlow–Kilkenny and Kilkenny–Waterford. That then allowed us to back-engineer accommodation and food, and to contact local media outlets to promote the walk. Pieta House organised their Darkness into Light committees in each town to welcome us - and quite a few of them ended up walking with us, which was fantastic. The buy-in really was something, and it ultimately made carrying the washing machine less of a burden.

On 21 December, I posted the walk schedule online and wrote the following:

> 'Was so afraid to publish. Let the journey begin. Any help/advice welcome. Getting the word out is a great help. Thanks to all who've liked and shared.'

A goal is a dream but when you post a goal or go public with it, there's so much more that goes with that: the declaration of effort, the prospect of failure but also the aspiration of achieving something, of hopefully making a meaningful mark. Of making a difference. The windows have been opened. The light has been let in. The word was now out there, beyond my inner circle. I'd stated what I was going to do. Now I had to go and do it.

Fast forward nine months to my sitting in the Europa Hotel in Belfast. I'm having breakfast prior to the *'Grand Départ'*, and that Facebook post is running through my mind.

I'm trying to eat but I can't avoid a sense of growing upset and tension. For the guts of a year, I've been telling all and sundry about all the training I've been doing, why I've trained the way I have and what it's all been for. It's part of this greater challenge, this 'bear' as I've described this obstacle that I'm determined to overcome, and I was going to hurt this bear so badly. But as I stood up from the breakfast table, standing in a doorway of the Europa, it hit me. I was now in the cave. The bear was standing broadside across the exit and he's asking me: 'And you said you were going to do what, exactly?' But I knew I'd miles to go before I'd sleep that particular day, and that the only thing I could carry with me that day to Banbridge was the washing machine. It wasn't a case of clicking my fingers and telling the bear to buzz off, but I had to find a very large filing cabinet to lodge him into before I began walking. The last time I checked, he's still locked in there, growling loudly in a cranny of what was once Europe's most heavily bombed hotel.

Putting myself out there, promoting the walk on Facebook and taking to the roads with the washing machine on my back was all done with a view to making a positive difference in people's lives, my own included. It prompted me to post the lyrics of 'Hope' by the Dixie Chicks. Below that, I simply wrote: 'Good morning. Please invite your friends to like this page.' Over 1,800 people liked that post, and I was beginning to feel like I was onto something special. The online reception was topping up the fuel I needed to see me through those tougher training sessions, as sweat fell like rain from my temple.

My natural inclination to become obsessed with things happened really rapidly when it came to Facebook. On a trip to Santa's Grotto in Waterford, I met the big guy's best-known representative in the city, the magnificently bearded Geno Kavanagh. I approached Geno to appear in a brief video on the Facebook page to promote the walk, which he agreed to without hesitation. And talk about the magic of Christmas, by the end of that same day we had 400 new likes for the page! That left me smiling broadly and I felt like I was really getting into the social media swing of things.

There are now over 5,000 people following my Facebook page, which may not be in the big league as far as other charities and businesses are concerned, but nonetheless it appears to be both helping and working.

A person in industry said as much to me and suggested the reason it's proven relatively popular was down to me 'telling a story and telling it honestly. People latch on to stories like that. There's no fakery about what you're doing, how you're doing it and what you're saying. And people have clearly been drawn to that.' So I kept the drum beating on that particular front, frequently posting messages of hope including 'Reach Out', 'Speak Out' and 'You're Not Alone' to name but three. And it eventually registered that I had to explain why I'd chosen to support Pieta House by carrying a washing machine down the east coast of Ireland. So that I did in the following post:

'Why a washing machine, many people have asked. It's symbolic of people carrying a heavy load in life, hopefully will grab media attention, the public will get interest and thereby generate loads of money.'

And then I posted cheekily that the machine had plenty of sponsors and a text number, neither of which we had at the time! But I was hopeful that would right itself in time. By Christmas Day, the page was up to 500 likes, and I was absolutely thrilled that the message had already reached so many different households. Added to that, highlighting both the walk but, more significantly, the work of Pieta House, exposed me to the reality of other people's sufferings and journeys. I wanted people unaffected by suicide and self-harm to develop some understanding of how pervasive an issue this is across so many households and communities, and that society as a whole needed to take ownership of the issue and collectively do something to make matters better by saving people's lives. There are two ways of spreading light: to be the candle, or be the mirror that reflects it – this was among the many messages I posted on the page, putting out a call which, to my absolute delight, has resonated with so many people.

The business of raising money had to be addressed, so I organised a big night at the Tower Hotel in Waterford city centre, which, for me, represents a momentous night in this whole endeavour. I'd never been involved in an event like this before, let alone organise one, but again, like the Facebook page, the support we received on the night proved an absolute head-spinner in the best possible sense. Gerry Duffy, a remarkable endurance athlete and public speaker, agreed to top the bill, where he would speak about his life and how embracing exercise transformed his life for the better.

The night itself raised around €1,500, but it also represented the first time I'd ever stood in front of my own kids and many friends and spoken about my own difficulties, my own mental health and depression. It was as big a step for me as any I'd subsequently take with the washing machine strapped to my back. But to able to stand before most of my inner circle and tell them publicly that I was in a better place was an admission I was so thrilled to share. Facebook's messaging power is fantastic – but try filling a room with people you love and speaking openly and honestly: the revelation of it.

The following day, I posted: 'Once you choose hope, anything is possible.' I just wanted people to realise that even if you are in the crappiest of places, there is always a way out. I got out, admittedly, not entirely, but I'm far enough away from the foul stuff to smell the roses nowadays. I see the value of having the love and support of my family and friends, and, even if it's a concept a lot of Irish people still struggle with, I recognise the value in me, in my life and how I've chosen to live it. And if I could get out of my own trough, then I know it's within the capability of so many others to do likewise. My addictive personality was being put to positive, life-affirming use. I couldn't contemplate failing. So I trained and I trained and I trained. I kept pumping the message out there via the Facebook page, and more and more people were getting in touch with me to share their own stories. More and more people joined in on my training walks. The magic was rippling outwards.

My daughter ran a fashion show at the Tower Hotel, completely off her own bat, and raised a few grand into the bargain. I was so thrilled by what she'd done for me: I had wondered what she'd make of me standing in a hotel room, in front of her, telling the wider world about my mental health difficulties. How the kids were going to react to me exposing pretty much all of my weaknesses to a wider audience had given me pause aplenty for thought. But they weighed in behind me, pushing me further down the road, both literally and metaphorically.

By April 2015, I was involved in my first photoshoot to promote the walk with the then Rose of Tralee, Maria Walsh: me, in a photoshoot – with a real photographer. Sucking the gut in and smiling was to become as much a part of my life as the washing machine itself, which was also taking on a personality of its own as Belfast drew nearer. The wildness of the task and the oddity of my choice of walking companion added to the growing sense of fun about it all, as far as the general public was concerned. By then, the text line was also up and running – 'Text PH4 to 50300' – and it soon became a mantra, I couldn't meet people without saying it. Like a Jehovah on speed, I was handing out cards to everyone I'd meet, be it on a night out or at a fundraiser, detailing the route of the walk and why I was doing it, and the magic kept rippling.

By then, I was out in public, training with the washing machine affixed to my back. Now, teachers are meant to be conservative types soaked in vanilla, but here I was, Mr O'Doherty, in the city I live and work in, heading out my front door with a washing machine affixed to me. The first walk took place at 10 p.m. I didn't want too many people seeing me. I walked to the end of our cul-de-sac and back – no more than two to three minutes – and I dashed back into the house, well, if one can ever dash with a large white good flung across you. But in that space of time, two of my neighbours saw me and both queried: 'What the hell are you doing, Enda?' It's a question I'd face a few more times thereafter, but I really began to embrace such a line of questioning.

The very first time I hit the Outer Ring Road with the washing machine, a car pulled in and the driver came over to me. We were walking towards a halting site at the time, which hadn't even dawned on me; she assumed we were Travellers and that we were bringing home something we'd only just bought from an electrical store down the road. I explained what we were doing and she nearly fainted in front of me! It turned out to be an RTÉ reporter, who then ran back to her car, took out her microphone and chatted with me there and then. And that helped to spread the word a little more.

Early morning walks each weekend became part and parcel of my preparation – and I wasn't alone. Anne Sinnott, a scout leader, joined us, as did past pupils Daire Grant and Liam Maher, and we'd be on our feet for anything between six and seven hours, clocking in between 15 and 20 miles. Their support was great. Their company was even better.

On 18 April 2015, as we were setting off from our meeting point at the Uluru Bar, on Waterford's leafy Dunmore Road, a woman from Clonmel popped out of her car and asked could she join us. We were delighted to have an additional member joining our walking group for the morning and off we went, and she walked with us for the six-plus hours we were out there. As we talked, she soon disclosed that she had lost her husband to suicide. There had been no warnings, no outward signs of his being in any way troubled. He took his life and broke her heart, and it really impacted upon me. At one point during the walk, the chat broke off, which was unusual given how well the conversation had flowed up until then. So I asked why she'd gone so quiet, to which she replied: 'Well, there's no way you could know this, so don't feel bad, but we've just walked past the spot where my husband took his life.' The reality facing so many families hit me between the eyes in that moment. It was tough. Very tough. Similar conversations would be had with a few more of our walking group in the weeks before we travelled to Belfast.

As the weeks went on and further stories were shared, the burden of carrying a washing machine was welcomingly diminished. I wasn't training to fail. I was determined not to fail. And on the wettest of days, we just kept walking. Maeve kept me going. The kids kept me going. Our walking group kept me going. The Facebook messages kept me going. The stories kept me going. The load was being shared, and that made everything easier.

Now all I had to do was walk from Belfast to Waterford with a washing machine strapped to my back.

2

Roots and Tremors

I grew up in the village of Dunlavin in west Wicklow, son of Tom and Theresa, and brother to Fiona and Karl. My parents ran a supermarket there and gave the three of us an idyllic childhood. Fantastic, warm and loving people. But from an early age, I had the feeling that I didn't quite fit in. For want of a better means of expressing this, a lot of my friends in Dunlavin were 'planters'. The village that I grew up in, where a monument to the 1798 Rebellion stands, is still effectively owned by a Scottish landlord and to this day locals still pay ground rent for their houses, a small sum it may be, yet they still have to pay it. That didn't sit well with me then, nor does it now. Idyllic and all as it was, I was bullied from quite an early age. My parents were perceived as being wealthy, and for no reason other than the fact that they happened to be running a local business, this apparently made me the 'wealthy kid' and that in turn put me in the firing line. That torrid time in my life left a mark, yet it wasn't the only childhood experience that traumatised me.

Towards the end of my time in primary school, my dad was involved in a car crash in which he almost lost his own life. I don't think I ever fully resolved that incident, causing a psychological ripple which, in my case, oscillated for many years. Nowadays, if a child of 11 or 12 was trying to come to terms with an issue similar to mine, a parent would more than likely seek out help for their child. But this was the 1970s. Sure you just got on with things, because that's what everyone did. In my early teens, I had to face down two further traumas: both robberies. Men broke into the front of our house, wielding sledgehammers, and proceeded to help themselves to the 'old reliables' – cigarettes and alcohol. I managed to load two cartridges into a gun and then invited the crooks to leave the premises, while my father also loaded and pointed his own gun in their direction as they made their exit through a window. It might read like primetime drama but for someone on the fringe of adolescence, there was no fun in arming a gun, even if part of me felt those bastards deserved nothing other than chests full of buckshot. Like most things in my life, I managed to cope and just get on with life in the immediate aftermath, but I suffered from the repercussions of that robbery. And the way in which I failed to truly grapple with these incidents augmented that sense that I was that little bit different to everyone else, that I didn't fit in.

A couple of years later, my parents were mugged on Grafton Street and I was literally in the middle of it. We had to fight off the people who were mugging them, another horrific experience. I don't know why anyone would want to harm my parents, the two kindest and warmest people I'd ever known prior to meeting Maeve. Shortly after that, during a college night out, this one particular guy, a total stranger, just sat down in front of me and smashed my face in, breaking my nose. I never saw it coming.

These traumas were beginning to pile up, and for the life of me I couldn't figure out which ladder I'd walked under, such was the level of misfortune which befell my parents, and then myself. But I chose to simply brush the totality of these events under the carpet, leaving them unresolved and undiscussed. Then I started drinking and before too long, I thought I'd found a way out of the trauma, when all I did was assume squatter's rights inside a bottle. But I was getting up to all sorts of crazy and loving it all. I never realised how imprisoned I was by alcohol until I said 'enough' and opted to escape. Downing 15 pints before a rugby international was nothing. Hundreds of pounds invested in a blur. Thankfully, my love of rugby was not exclusively tied up in the gargle. I regularly attend Leinster matches nowadays and the boys in blue remain one of my great passions, but once the full-time whistle blows at the RDS, I now make for the car, rather than the pub, and within two hours I'm back in my own bed. The contentment of it.

Such levels of contentment weren't something I could have envisaged in those early days of sobriety. I never considered myself to be an alcoholic while I was drinking. I only really reached that conclusion once I stopped. And those first six sleep-deprived months, with no drink in my bloodstream, were tortuous. Imagine someone inserting 5,000 ants under your skin and the skin then crawling off your body: that's what it felt like every day for those six months. I remember sitting in the bathroom at 2 a.m. and checking my phone to figure out the exact moment of sunrise because that's when I knew the nightmares would stop. I woke up four or five times most nights screaming, my bedsheets soaked by my sweat, with my body in total shock.

I've spoken to some medical people about that time in my life and they quickly concluded that I went about getting sober in entirely the wrong way. At my consumption levels, I needed medication and counselling; I sought no medical advice at all, which was absolutely crazy. As for attending AA meetings? Sure those people were all drunks, they were total losers. Why would I have wanted any truck with those deadbeats? The thought of standing up and telling a bunch of strangers, 'Hi, I'm Enda and I'm an alcoholic' had no appeal whatsoever to this particular alcoholic. Looking back, what I did was very dangerous and I realise in hindsight how lucky I was to emerge from that haze. There is no shame in seeking help, whatever your trauma or poison of choice may be. I can see that now. I couldn't then. That's addiction for you. But I got through it and somehow kept functioning. You never really know what's going on in someone's life, be it what's in their heart, what's in their head or, often critically, what's not there.

One afternoon at De La Salle, I went for a walk with a very kind colleague; she could see I was in bad shape. 'Enda, what's going on?' she asked me. And those words were like an old-fashioned camera bulb exploding in front of me. I opened up. I told her that for the previous two months, every time I closed my eyes I saw my own memorial card. I saw the other side. I saw the world without me in it and for a time that was the only way I saw out of alcoholism. It still freaks me out.

I never attempted suicide but I recall walking along the Dunmore Road one afternoon and seeing a huge truck coming towards me, and the thought of stepping off the footpath and in front of that truck appealed to me. It was going to hurt me a lot, but it was going to give such relief from the way I was feeling. It felt like a means of escape, a way of getting my head back onto a soft pillow. I thought about the release it would bring. And bear in mind this all transpired after I stopped drinking. Now, I'd experienced extreme anxiety when I was 19 which rendered me speechless - my tongue had enflamed - so I went to the local doctor and was told this had been brought on by both my college exams and the lifestyle I was living. But this was an altogether different feeling. An altogether more debilitating feeling. Yet I still found a way to cope and despite my desire to drink, I know if I went back there, it wouldn't be a truck on the Dunmore Road that would take my own lights out. Alcohol just isn't an option for me anymore. It can't be, although I'm still amazed I've not had even a mouthful for almost a dozen years.

I still have bad dreams nowadays but I no longer wake up screaming. I can regulate my breathing and quell a panic attack inside a minute. Anxiety doesn't rule me the way it used to; of course I still get anxious but I generally know the way out now, so much so that such moments have been reduced to blips. The triggers are there, but I've learned to minimalise their excesses, which really comes into play during those weeks where I could have three or four evening presentations somewhere up the country, with a day's teaching to follow. When I get overtired, I know it will happen, but there's an element of safety at play because I'll know when anxiety will strike, it no longer creeps up on me like a Grafton Street mugger. I can deal with it now.

There were so many things in my life that I was unaware of for so long; chief among them was my mental health and how I dealt with my emotions. But both were clouded in alcohol and when you're unaware of your anxiety, your depression, your alcoholism, you can't see what's sometimes plain to others. So how can you expect to find a way out when you don't even realise that's what you need above everything else?

The difference with my addictions nowadays is that they're all productive. All of them shape me positively and have helped to improve my life, and I don't beat myself up any more. After all, it's very hard for anyone else to like you if you don't like yourself. I've got my quirks. I know I've got my faults and I know there are times when I am a total pain in the arse. But on the whole, I'm Tom and Theresa's son. The boy from Dunlavin. Tom and Theresa's son is off the drink and really enjoying his life and his world is all the better for it. I'm determined to keep it that way. Why? There's just too much living to do.

3

Enda 2.0

'Once, years ago, a crowd of us were going along the Shepherd's Bush Road when out of a lane came a chap with a donkey - just the sort of donkey and just the sort of cart that they have at home. He came out quite suddenly and abruptly and we all cheered him. Nobody who has not been an exile will understand me, but I stand for that.'

Michael Collins, *The Big Fellow*[2]

I'm an early riser, as is Maeve. Talk about relationship goals. Between teaching and the motivational speeches which have become part and parcel of what it is to be me now - Enda 2.0 - being fed, watered and 'spun' (as in a spin class at my local gym) before zigzagging between classrooms, the staff room and meeting rooms of De La Salle College, is par for the course. I'm ready to take on the world while most of one hemisphere is still cocooned under a duvet.

On a typical day, even during a teacher's allegedly favourite time of the year, the summer holidays, the 5-a.m. start levels me. It's an adrenaline shot. The early morning chat with Maeve is infinitely more enjoyable than reaching for the snooze button in a hungover haze before enduring another day, and I knew quite a few of those mornings prior to the 'refit'.

After the 5-a.m. kick-off, the pre-dawn conflab with Maeve, the spin class, bounding up the lofty steps of De La Salle, pumped that I've emptied myself on the bike already, I know I may not disengage from the happy tornado that life has become these past few years for the next 12 to 13 hours. But I'm completely fine with that. My addictive tendencies didn't vanish when I made the decision to get sober. It hasn't worked like that for me and I doubt that's the case for most addicts. Getting hooked on life wasn't something I'd banked on when I realised I had to take another path. Yet here I am. And life is bloody good. It really is. But it's taken a while to get there.

Addiction is structure. It's something by its very definition you tend to do every day. It's like happiness or faith. It's something most of us can relate to on some abstract level. It feels practical when you're consumed by it – I guess we're back in tornado territory here – but there wasn't an overwhelming sense of chaos for me in the middle of that storm, because this was the time in my life when my entire world revolved around alcohol.

Enda 1.0, the old me, used to go to a lot of Waterford United matches. Since I stopped drinking, I haven't been inside the gates of the Regional Sports Centre on a Friday night. Not once. The match was largely immaterial. It became an excuse to drink: having a few pints before the match, having a naggin during the match, then washing it all down with a few more pints after the full-time whistle. And the next day was pure hair-of-the-dog stuff. That was normality as I saw it at the time. That was living.

For me, alcohol was a crawling disaster. It infected me. It affected me. It threw me off course and became the fork-tailed imp on my shoulder.

> 'So what if it's Thursday night and you've a full day of teaching tomorrow? Why wait for the end-of-week glass of wine when you can have a bottle tonight – and what about all those other days of the week you're not knocking them back. Why not mark an 'X' on every day of the week and just get pissed each and every day? Why wait until Friday? Why wait for a Blues match or a night out with herself? Sure isn't everyone more fun when they're jarred up?'

I listened to the imp. He might as well have been one of those TV evangelists in a heaving arena, telling me, the wide-eyed sucker in the auditorium, who has already stuck a ton in the preacher's pocket, that salvation was at hand, albeit for a sizeable 'just sign here' portion of my take-home pay. So what if the voice in my ear was branding me? And so it went. Enda 1.0: signed up for the piss-up 24/7, an apostle of 'sure whatever you're having', when what I needed in my life more than anything right then was to renounce that particular faith.

As an alcoholic, I couldn't have been dealt worse cards, which might sound odd since neither of my parents were similarly afflicted. But there's history and forbearance at work there, and, in time, I've learned to feed off that. My father would tell me he's pretty sure he would have gone full blown had he ever hit those tracks, but his mother died an alcoholic, as did her mother before her. Dad made the decision to stay off the tracks before that particular train ran right over him. He's remained a teetotaller his entire life.

And alcoholism was no stranger to my mother's side of the family either; her own father carried an imp on his shoulder. There's scarcely a threshold in the country that has escaped alcoholism and all of its aftershocks. We seem to be genetically predisposed to it. My grandmother owned a pub, which in hindsight was hardly a help. Had she run a sweetshop, she might have had a few more fillings than most but life might have been easier. But alcoholism finds a way of developing, rooting, transfusing and distorting a sense of normalcy. Most alcoholics, after all, aren't licensees and the DNA probably had my grandmother marked for addiction, one way or the other.

In my case, the 'Irish disease' first took hold of me in west Wicklow, aged 18, via our family off-licence – but hold me to further exploratory thought on that. I feel like we need to get to Kenya and its radioactive portaloos, a near-death experience, bowel beyond irritation and, as you do, a washing machine on my back for some non-alcoholic related context. Early rising, spin cycling, life-embracing Enda 2.0 needs to breathe, albeit with difficulty, on the slopes of Mount Kilimanjaro for a little while...

***

Late June 2017. I'm sat down for a pre-Pieta Challenge interview with my co-writer, Dermot Keyes, wearing his day-jobbing hat as a reporter with the *Munster Express* (a Waterford-based newspaper – he's since moved onto the *Waterford News & Star* where he's now deputy editor) and the coffee is flowing as freely as the chat. As I drain another piping mug, the draining slopes of Kilimanjaro are on my mind. All 19,343 feet of her. That's the equivalent of nine Slievenamons. And don't forget the six-and-a-half stone (40kg in new money) of additional washing machine that has to be hauled up the world's highest free-standing mountain.

Why Dermot? He met me just outside Mullinavat (14 kilometres from Waterford) for the final stretch of the Belfast to Waterford walk, which was also the first time we'd met face to face. He was kitted out in a Waterford GAA t-shirt, in addition to trainers, running gear and Lycra shorts, so he looked the part given the day that was in it. But he also spoke to me like a man who had grasped the motivation behind my walk. I spoke to a lot of journalists that week but none of them listened to me the way Dermot did. There was an intensity in his eyes and a palpable sense of enthusiasm both for what I was doing and for his own brief on that sunny afternoon in south Kilkenny, which ultimately led us all across Rice Bridge and back into my adopted home city. Dermot was instantly friendly, engaging, positive and clearly intelligent, and struck me as a man who doesn't do things by halves – a trait he owes to his late father, Johnny, he'd later tell me.

When we shook hands on the Quay, saying our goodbyes as the crowds of friends and well-wishers began to disperse, I felt like I'd not only made a friend but someone I could work with. So when the idea of committing my story to print germinated, Dermot felt like a natural choice for me: a well-heeled reporter with over 20 years of experience, a great deal of which he has spent listening to people willing to share their stores with him. So I called him, pitched the book to him and he immediately boarded the good ship O'Doherty. Wednesday morning interviews prior to the first class bell sounding at De La Salle College soon became the norm. They quickly developed a rhythm of their own. 'Right Enda, I'm going to ask one question and pretty much just sit back for the hour', he'd regularly intone, followed by a hearty laugh.

But Dermot never sat back during any of those conversations. He manically jotted down thoughts into his Moleskine journal while we spoke, sometimes running to several heavily inked pages with particular phrases underlined and speech-bubbled while I spoke. He drew perspectives out of me I had not anticipated sharing with him, thoughts which regularly drew my emotions unexpectedly to the surface. I'd face into my working day emotionally drained but utterly convinced that I had picked the right partner to tell this story with. I can't imagine ever arguing with Dermot. He's a decent guy, an honest man who has no tolerance for bullshit and a damn fine journalist. He's also another friend I'd never have made had it not been for the washing machine.

Even rattling off the numbers for the climb in my head makes the 379 kilometres walked with the washing machine between Belfast and Waterford two summers previously feel like a routine stroll. Given that I had not been able to travel abroad for altitude training – the funds didn't stretch that far – taking on this particular Pieta Challenge represented a genuine and literal step into the unknown. But I've put down 400 days of training before boarding the flight bound for Addis Abbaba. In the six weeks leading up to the trip, I've been working out for between two and three hours every day. Addiction remains structure for Enda 2.0, only the fix has been re-routed.

The pre-Kilimanjaro MOT read-out is a mixed bag: my heart and lungs are A1; the boobs are like concrete and the shoulders feel capable of getting through the trek. I'm like a small ox – but there's a few chinks in the armour, even if I'm doing my best to channel Hugh Jackman on the body-building front. But what I wouldn't give for Wolverine's healing powers right now.

I strained my left knee a few weeks back. I've got tendonitis, my IT band is quite sore and I'm pretty sure I've a tear in my meniscus too. I'm not broadcasting it to the outside world right now, but I'm down to a leg and a half before the thinner air of the mountain is even up one nostril. It's not the scenario I had in mind when embarking on this latest epic. But there will be plenty of fit and muscly 20- and 30-year-olds heading up Kilimanjaro with me and I'm not foolish enough to think it's just going to me with the washing machine all the way up.

Given that I'm not too keen on dying any time soon, I realise at some stage during this challenge, a medical team member may have to cry 'halt' into my half-listening ear. After all, you don't see too many concussed rugby players volunteering for an early shower, so I realise the ultimate decision won't be mine to make if it comes to that. I've had to face my weaknesses down before, but it's best to park that until that moment potentially arises. What will be, will be. But I really want to reach that summit and unfurl a tricolour.

Kilimanjaro. Eight days of upward hiking, every day of which you're losing oxygen. The last night of the hike will involve hiking for 17 hours, much if it in darkness, at minus 20 degrees with 40 per cent oxygen. It's a Bond villain's evil lair without the convenient escape plan reveal during the third act. I've not had real-time altitude training, and that's still a nagging concern, but using the oxygen mask while training at Waterford Institute of Technology has at least given me a semblance of what lies ahead of me.

So why do this? Why take on something that might kill me or someone else among the 35-strong group that have raised €4,000 each to take part in this adventure?

I'm driven by a couple of things. There's the fear of failure as well as the fear of dying on the mountain. I realise there are a lot of people around Ireland who are going to follow this challenge and depend on it for hope and inspiration. The training has been multiple times harder than it was in terms of Belfast to Waterford – there'll be no four- or five-star hotels either – and there is nowhere to hide if I lose control of my bowels this time.

The mobile home for the trek is a sleeping bag and a tent, while grub will be whatever we can boil on a campfire, and I know that those elements alone represent a real challenge in itself. I don't like the dark and I'm a bit claustrophobic: I clearly like making things as tough as possible! But, even down to a leg and a half, I know I'm much better prepared than I was two years ago. But all of that is small potatoes.

Ten people will die by suicide in Ireland this week yet where's the State campaign to reverse this trend? The Road Safety Authority's campaigns are clearly working: there are fewer people dying in motor-related accidents now than there were back in the late 70s when we had a hell of lot fewer cars on the roads – and that's absolutely fantastic.

But where's the State's Life Safety Authority? Why have successive governments failed to grasp this nettle? If they had, we wouldn't need Pieta House, the Samaritans or Aware the way we do today. We wouldn't need sober alcoholics walking and climbing in all manner of places to tell people it's okay to not feel okay; that there are ways and means of sharing the load, that things can get better.

A lot of people thought me walking from Belfast to Waterford with the washing machine was a crazy idea and that it wouldn't catch on, and I was told Pieta House wouldn't expand or ever open in Waterford. But I've always relished being told that something can't be done. And here we are. Pieta House is open at the Waterside, near Waterford city centre, and people are getting help locally, which is fantastic.

I carried the washing machine from Belfast to Waterford. I was so determined to do so. The same thought process applied to hiking Kilimanjaro. The core of both challenges was to spread a positive mental health message, to 'Share the Load'. Life can and will get better if you reach out, and I'll never grow weary of sharing that message with anyone. And that's why I've carried a cumbersome white good on my back on both Irish and African soil.

4

The Sporty Type

Growing up in Dunlavin, badminton was the must-play sport. Everyone in the village played it, be you man, woman, child or goldfish! Ascending to the ranks of the senior town team was the biggest sporting goal that us kids of the early 1970s aspired to. A gang of us played the game and we received coaching from the Peard family, who were to Dunlavin in badminton terms what the Wright Brothers are to aviation. Mr Peard Snr was an All-England Badminton champion and his son Mark had played for Ireland, while his wife had represented England. The Peards knew their stuff – and then some – and we young Dunlavinites were the grateful recipients of their expertise.

The standard of coaching was probably the equal of any available in Ireland at the time and we honed our skills in the hall, which, fortunately for me, was right next door to our supermarket. We actually kept the key to the hall in the shop, which meant I could pop in and out when it suited me, and that's when my OCD first began to manifest itself: if I wanted to go in and practice serving or just bound up and down the hall, I could. And I enjoyed the application, the perspiration and the isolation of working out on my own, before joining in the subsequent training session with my team mates. The physical bug was beginning to bite, and my competitive instincts also began to emerge, and we won an All-Ireland title at the Community Games, which was an enormous thrill.

On our triumphant return home from Mosney, we were greeted by the sight of blazing bonfires on the crests of several nearby hills, as we were transported into the village on the back of a truck. Talk about a

Kodak moment. In fact, that medal still takes pride of place in the middle of the mantelpiece in our sitting room in Waterford. It means a lot to me and that success remains a treasured childhood memory, which provided me with my first major realisation about what can be achieved through hard work, diligent training and self-belief. I subsequently ended up making a couple of (provincial) Leinster teams, and moving a further rung up the representative ladder got me dreaming about playing the sport at semi-professional level. But my parents, while utterly supportive of my sporting endeavour, were as realistic as they were practical. And so my dream of going semi-pro fell by the wayside while I busied myself with secondary school life at Newbridge Dominican College. But I have to say I absolutely loved my time there. I went on to play rugby to a pretty high level during my time at Newbridge, even if my career began quite accidentally.

In First Year, we were told in no uncertain terms that if your name appeared on a list for rugby training and you subsequently didn't turn up, you'd be in big trouble – let's not forget that corporal punishment was still in vogue at the time.

Keen as I was to avoid a hiding, I dutifully turned up when 'E O'Doherty' was printed on a sheet for junior rugby one Monday morning. I pulled on my gear and was ready to go, blissfully unaware that the notification was for an Edward O'Doherty who was three years my senior! But as things turned out, I held my own on the field as my accidental rugby rise first took flight. I was five feet nine inches and weighed twelve and a half stone. From second centre, I was, primarily, a destructive force: I wasn't great with the ball but boy was I good at hurting people! My mother came to one game I played against Blackrock College: my inflicting physical pain on a litany of opponents didn't go down too well with her. She missed the whole reason for my being at number 13. I wasn't there to paint. I was there to detonate and I loved the big hits. I thrived on the aggression that life in the three-quarter line demanded of me.

Unfortunately, when playing a pre-Christmas match in Third Year I fractured a vertebra. I hit the ground really hard and a few players, along with the referee, asked me if I was okay. I assured the interested parties that all was well. The referee then asked me if I could stand up, to which I replied: 'Of course I can.' But as I attempted to rise, I realised I'd no feeling in my legs. And rather than think that I was in a serious spot of bother, my first thought was: 'Crap, my mother is going to kill me.' And while the vertebra healed, that was the end of my rugby career, but it was body-slamming fun while it lasted. And that was pretty much the end of things for me on the adolescent sporting front, as I platform-dived into cider, vodka and brandy for more years than I now care to recall. Alcoholism is partly genetic and I was clearly born with some genes but I fed those genes through my own negative activity – through my own behaviour. I mean you don't wake up one day and consider yourself an alcoholic. It's not married to geometry or any known metric. It's ivy-like, snaking into your system, insipidly tightening like a vice.

For the better part of six years, I didn't compete in any sport at any level; my senses numbed by vodka and orange (my first ever drink, for the record), followed by brandy and milk and many, many pints. Come 1990, when I arrived at De La Salle College to begin my teaching career, I met a teacher named Jean Brosnan, who asked me if I played any sport, which led to my recalling my golden, Peard-inspired past in badminton. She asked me would I play for the De La Salle team, who were then in white-hot opposition to the city's other badminton club, based on Lady Lane in the city centre. Two nights later, on a Wednesday, I found myself in a car with Pat Walsh, Martin Molloy, Barry Kennedy and Jean: 30 years later, all five of us remain good friends – Martin even climbed Kilimanjaro with me. We did the egg-and-onion sandwich circuit all over Waterford and further afield, and it was a great way of getting back into sport.

But my undisputed re-exposure to competitive sport came about when Maeve showed me a 'Couch to 5K' piece in a magazine she'd bought. You probably know the gig: run 30 seconds, walk 30 seconds and so on. 'I'll never do that on my own,' she said. 'Maybe you'd do it with me?' So off we went, running 30 seconds, walking 30 seconds over and over and over, and from that beginning, Maeve ended up running a half-marathon. We ran the Belfast Marathon together – and somewhere in the middle of that, I took on my first triathlon, the 'Hook or by Crook' event at Dunmore East, which I later discovered is the hardest sprint triathlon in Ireland. The hills! Oh, those unforgiving hills. The best thing that I can say about it is that I survived it.

During the 750-metre swim, somebody hit me in the back of the head and pushed me down below the waterline and I panicked. I had a panic attack in the water and began to wave at the emergency boat. But I'd gone out so fast that the boatman was naturally more interested in the slower swimmers behind me and therefore closer to him and far likelier to run, well, swim into trouble. I was having troubling drawing breath and came closer than I have at any time in my adulthood to soiling myself, such were my fear levels. By the time the emergency boat became aware of me, I'd calmed myself down enough to finish the swim. My subsequent endurance experiences with the washing machine might never have come about had that emergency boatman seen me in a state of panic just 300 metres into the swim. Thereafter, my addictive tendencies and my ambition to do better really came to the surface. I needed a better bike. I had to get better runners. I had to go further, and then a little further after that.

My evolution as a triathlete, as it was put to me, was unheard of, bordering on crazy. In the space of three months, I went from finishing a sprint event to completing a Half Ironman in Kerry, and it was well named – The Lost Sheep – because that's what I resembled for a few days afterwards. It was draining and featured two Category One climbs, the Healy Pass and the Caha Pass, but I got through both, and I was very proud of that. So by end of my first summer literally back in the saddle, I had completed a Sprint, an Olympic, a Double Olympic and a Half Ironman. It was, to be frank, stupid but hey, this is me!

At work, a good colleague of mine, Paul Ogle, a former Waterford senior footballer who is now a top-class Ironman triathlete, in addition to another colleague and triathlete, Mick Brett, both encouraged me to look upon The Lost Sheep as a competitive stepping stone and they were right. It convinced me that I could cope with such a physical and mental workload, and I gained enormous benefit from being in the company of like-minded people when it came to getting moving again. Paul and Mick were so encouraging. Now they saw a fear in me, which was pretty understandable for someone taking on a daunting challenge, but they also saw an energy and a determination to succeed. And the journey towards Ironman changed everything.

The Ironman day is truly awesome: a 4-kilometre swim, a 180-kilometre cycle and the cherry on top: a full marathon. The iron required on race day was forged in the 10 months (two hours daily) leading up to the start-er's gun. The big day itself is essentially a victory lap. And with The Lost Sheep box ticked, I felt I wanted to take things to the next level. But it was Maeve who once again provided me with the toe in the derriere I needed to take that giant leap. She was correcting Leaving Cert exam papers and I popped down to the study, where she was working her way through the papers, to see how she was getting on. She broke away from her work and spoke to me like Jedi Master Yoda did to Luke Skywalker on Dagobah. 'Stop letting fear control you.' She produced a credit card from her pocket and told me: 'Go and enter that race. Stop putting it off. Stop worrying about it. Just do it.'

I went upstairs, logged onto the Ironman UK website and paid the £500, which was a sizeable wad to hand over, and that was before flights, accommodation, physio, the bike, other equipment and the training itself came into consideration. Ten months later, I was stood on the start line at Pendleton, a collapsed coal mine outside Bolton in Lancashire, among a field of 2,500 people. It was 5 a.m., and 'God Save the Queen' was blaring. Standing in that lake, with elbows rubbing elbows, all gunning for 10 flags at the same time, it's like the worst bar fight you've ever been in, while whirring in, you guessed it, a washing machine. And as the sun came up and the British anthem played, I wondered: what the hell was I doing here? I was surrounded by lean machines whereas I had a body shape somewhere between Lions' centres Scott Gibbs and Rob Henderson, but I was as determined as anyone in that water. Well, possibly not.

Nursing a niggly calf, I felt a bump from behind me as I walked towards the swim, so I nudged back, only to be met by a further nudge. I turned around, to see one contestant carrying his friend into the water. The man being carried had no legs: he'd lost them both while serving in Afghanistan. It was a great lesson to me, and didn't half put manners on me when it came to my troublesome calf. At least I still had both of mine. It was important not to sweat on the incidentals. I ended up racing along-side this double amputee for a good 14 miles during the marathon, and this was despite blood seeping from both his stumps as we approached the hallway mark, which he had to bandage up. Without undue fuss, he cleaned his wounds and 20 minutes later, as my fatigue levels rose, he passed me. Talk about an ironman.

The cut-off point to complete the entire event was 17 hours but within that there are three individual cut-off points for each discipline: you've got to be out of the water in two hours, so the prospect of being hauled out of the race in front of your family and friends is a real risk. You can be taken out of the water or off the road, meaning no finish for you – a horrendous way of bookending a 10-month preparatory block.

Four-and-a-half hours into the bike ride, I realised I was in a race against the cut-off point. A physical low tends to catalyse emotional weakness and I was having a really bad time on the bike. I was coming up Sheepshank Hill, a quite famous hill in the locality. I was on my own and I was crying, full bubble-snot style. I was in physical pain, brimming with self-pity and felt destined for failure. An awful landmark beckoned, as did another black cloud. Quite silently, a pleasant Canadian (is there any other kind?) cycled up alongside me and asked if I was okay. 'I'm not bloody okay, no,' said I, attempting to wipe away some of the mucus and spittle coating my chin. He embarked on a conversation with me, which went something like this.

Pleasant Canadian (PC): 'Why did you sign up for this?'

Enda O'Doherty (EOD): 'To finish the Ironman. I wanted to get fit.'

PC: 'I'm really sorry but I'm not buying that. Nobody gives up a year of their life and spends this amount of money just to get in shape. Come on, tell me. Why are you really doing this?'

EOD: 'Okay then. Well, I've got three kids and I've never wanted them to think that their dad is ordinary. And when I'm gone, I want them all to think that their dad was something else. It's really important for me to set an example to them.'

PC: 'Right, that's good, but I still don't think that's why you're doing it.'

EOD: 'It is, I'm telling you.'

PC: 'I'm not deliberately being a pain in the ass here, but I still don't think that's the real reason. Look at you, look how emotional you are. You've clearly put a lot of yourself, probably all of yourself, in to get to this point. This is not just about doing something for your kids.'

EOD: 'Okay. Fair enough. Look, my wife is with my kids at the finish line. She's a beautiful person, inside and out. She's wonderful, she's intelligent, has incredible integrity and is just the most decent person I know. I've never met anyone else like her. She doesn't talk negatively about anything or anybody. Within two days of meeting her, I asked Maeve - that's her name - to marry me. I knew how special she was the minute I met her. So it's really important to me to show to her that her man is capable of something different and that I'm not just like most other husbands.'

PC: 'Right, now I feel like we're getting towards some truth here, but I still think you're holding something back on me. Why are you really doing this? Come on, you're never going to see me again after this; we might not even see each other at the finish line. What's really going on here?'

EOD: 'Look. I'm an alcoholic. I've passed a pub three times on this loop and every time I've gone past it, I thought about pulling in there and knocking back a few pints to take the edge off me, because I'm on the edge here now at the moment, let me tell you! But in the last two hills here, I feel like I've been trying to cycle out of a bottle of brandy, that's what I've been seeing. That's what I've been feeling. And right now I'm running on empty.'

PC: 'Right. Okay, here's how I see it. You've got to keep pushing now. You've still got time on the bike if you don't give in. Try not to get too stressed, and keep thinking about who is waiting for you at the finish line.'

EOD: 'Okay, I'll try and do that. Do you mind me asking why you're doing this?'

PC: 'Well I came home from work one evening and my wife was in our living room, watching TV. She was sat there in the chair and she was dead. She died in front of the TV. She was in her early 30s. After she died, I lost my job and I nearly lost the house. I couldn't eat, I couldn't sleep, I really couldn't function like a regular human being and I was drinking too much. I lost the love of my life and my sanity, just about the worst two-in-one deal I can think of. One day, a friend visited me, now he was one of those guys who kept calling to see how I was; I opened the door and he was stood there with two bikes. "Come on," he said to me. "We're going for a bike ride". So I decided to go. I really couldn't believe what happened next. The bike triggered something in me, in my mind and in my body, and we rode for between two and three hours.

'When we got back to my house, my friend told me I should hold onto the bike and use it again if I ever felt like it. Within a few minutes of my friend leaving, I got back on the bike again and rode for another few hours. When I got back on the bike for the second time, I regained an appetite, so I ate whatever was in the fridge – which wasn't all that much because I wasn't going to the store too regularly – and then I slept properly for the first time in months. When I woke up the next morning, the feeling I'd got from being on the bike was still in my system. There was something good going on so I decided to go for another ride that day, and the day after, and the day after that. I've taken part in a few of these events now, but the first time I finished one of these, I felt as if my wife had given me permission to be happy again. I felt like she was smiling down on me, telling me it was okay to get back into the world and start living again. Ironman has saved my life. So you get to that finish line. You enjoy that moment.'

EOD: 'I will. I promise. Thanks. Good luck.'

PC: 'You too. Take care now.'

And away he pedalled. Sheepshank Hill had become my own road to Damascus. And I kept going.

Thankfully, about an hour into the marathon, I had another revelation. By that stage I was reduced to shuffling but I knew that I was going to make it inside the cut-off point, and it was the loveliest of mental realisations. It helped to stave off the worst effects of the single greatest fatigue I'd experienced to that point in my life. No matter what, my battered body was going to get there.

Inside the final two miles, I really felt like I was losing it, as I ran past a quite vocal spectator who looked and sounded so similar to TV petrol head Jeremy Clarkson. It was in fact TV petrol head Jeremy Clarkson; it turned out that his wife was shuffling towards the finish line in and around the same time as I was. This wasn't the sort of pace he was accustomed to getting shouty about but there he was as Mrs Clarkson and many more of us ambled towards deliverance. And then at last, at long, long last, there was the finishing chute. A big screen came into view and the public address bellowed: 'Enda O'Doherty, you are an Ironman.' And there they all were. My family. A huge hug. Tears. Unbridled relief. I'd done it. I'd really achieved something significant, and it wasn't just for me. A finish line is nothing without someone to celebrate it with, and to have the lads there waiting was just magical.

Initially, I'd not wanted the kids to come along, but Maeve thought they should see me that day, whatever the outcome was. She explained: 'If you fail, I want them to see how you deal with failure. But if you finish this, then I want us to celebrate it as a family together.' That single sentence encapsulated Maeve's love for me, her care and her wisdom. The happiness at that finish line will never leave me. The entire endeavour changed my entire life. Anything was possible. Everything. Even carrying a washing machine down the Irish eastern seaboard.

5

Belfast to Waterford – Part One

'The reality is that if your dream is to accomplish something awesome, it's not going to be easy. If it were easy, everyone would be doing it. People who go for greatness are going to get knocked down a lot. They'll have difficult times. They'll struggle with doubt and uncertainty. People around them will question the wisdom of their quest. The issue is not whether you'll fail, because you will. It's whether you'll get back up and keep going. It's whether you can sustain your self-confidence and your belief in yourself and keep bouncing back. Failure is only final when you stop striving.'

Dr Bob Rotella, *How Champions Think*[3]

I've always applied what I would describe as a 'funny logic' to life, which, to a great extent, explains why I've become synonymous with carrying an unyielding household appliance over vast distances. And that logic has sustained me through some tough times in my life, let alone through 20-mile training walks in the driving rain ahead of the trip to Belfast, the starting point for my inaugural Pieta Challenge.

When the Pieta Challenge assembled at De La Salle College prior to the spin to Belfast, I was really, really shocked when I arrived there, scanning the faces of so many people who had turned out to wish us well. And it took some time for me to register that most of the people I was looking at had come to know me through the Facebook page. The school car park was packed with vehicles and overflowing with kindness, which blew me away. I couldn't have envisaged a more heart-warming start to this adventure.

On our northerly drive we pit-stopped on the Sallins Road to say hello to Mam and Dad. Here I was, a 46-year-old adult about to embark on a never before undertaken adventure, and I still had to call into my mammy and daddy to show them the van with my picture emblazoned on the side of it. And as mad an idea as she thought it was and had told me so more than once, Mam still wanted her photo taken at the front of the house with Dad and the son, the 'Black Sheep', decorating a van! It's a moment I treasure all the more now since there's one less parent to call in on.

Conventional logic had led me to convince myself that I and I alone would carry the washing machine along Ireland's eastern seaboard. That same sentiment would subsequently apply on Kilimanjaro – but reality struck in both instances, and that pang first struck just outside Drogheda, three days into our walk. I was banjaxed, I realised I was going to have to share the load and I felt really bad about it. But then a voice (I can't remember who exactly) put me in my place, stating: 'Come on, Enda. Cop onto yourself. Share the load. Isn't that what this is all about?' I couldn't argue with that point. I was too tired to present a worthwhile counter-argument so I unstrapped myself from my 70lb walking companion, seeing its profile diminish on the road ahead of me, while the words of Bill Withers' 'Lean On Me' ran on a loop between my ears. I'd opted for wisdom. There was, after all, always tomorrow. And the idea of sharing the load myself during the walk mushroomed from that moment on.

Surreally, having just acceded visitation rights to the washing machine a matter of minutes previously, while walking briefly on my own, a guy pulled up alongside me and asked: 'Is that the washing machine man down there?' I was too tired by then and felt it was too complicated to explain what had just happened, so I replied: 'Yeah, that's him.' In reply, I was told: 'My goodness, that's a brilliant thing he's doing, sure Pieta House is a great charity. And here', handing me a €50 note out through the window, 'give that to him and tell him to keep going, will ya?' I assured him that the 'man himself' would get the money as he sped up and drove away. It was such a surreal moment, yet so wonderfully grat-ifying. And that donation really did help me to keep going right then, a timely reminder that this walk wasn't about me. It was about a cause. It was about helping people. It was about saving lives.

The seven-month training schedule had tested me on every level, and there were times in the build-up to Belfast when I did wonder what the hell I was at. The funny logic didn't always win out. There was one particular Saturday when we were 17 miles into a walk; the plan was to do 23, and those final six miles almost broke me. The route looped back towards our house but then veered away and back out towards Bally-gunner and we literally had to keep going until the watch bleeped. It was the first time that my feet had badly blistered and by the time I got home that evening I genuinely felt like I'd had enough.

The harness was starting to wear, it was getting narrower and narrower, and it was cutting into my clavicle on both sides. That night, in the shower, the stinging sensation of soapy water seeping into raw flesh, combined with a burning chest, left me in a very bad place. And as I hobbled out of the shower to dry myself off, the thought of taking on a 26-miler the following day filled me with dread.

A single 26-mile walk accounted for between six-and-a-half and seven hours, and I needed to attain a level of fitness where I'd get through up to 30 miles every day for eight consecutive days. In training I put in seven-hour sessions on both Saturdays and Sundays, and the first thing I did on Monday evenings once I got in from work was to throw the washing machine up on my back for two hours. There was nothing easy about any of it, but the support I received while out on the road and the feedback on my Facebook page helped to fuel the engine. It helped me to keep my eye on the prize and guided me through those rough patches. And as my physical strength grew, so too did my mental resilience.

When you spend seven hours talking to someone during a walk, there's so much going on, and not all of immediately evident. You're talking, enjoying the better part of one's waking day in the company of as many as 11 other people by choice, with only each other for distraction. And it was time we all put to good use, during which deep friendships developed. We developed a different level of knowledge, appreciation and affection for each other. It was the closest feeling I've ever had to being in camp as an active member of a team, each and every one of us striving to drive the other on in the expectation of delivering the optimum perfor-mance come 'Walk Week'. On the road, the group was there for me, looking after me, and that carried me through those eight gruelling days. This was team work on a level I'd never experienced previously, and it was magical.

Given the interest which the Facebook page had whipped up, there was a sense of having to keep the wider audience in the loop in terms of how we were doing, and built into that was the need to be 'on message'. We collectively concluded that no one logging in wanted to hear about how my bowels were performing so when it came to the video blogs which we posted, let's just say the editing process came into play. I felt it was important to transmit a positive message to everyone who had lent their support to us, so that's how we decided to spin it.

Arriving at the Europa Hotel the first day, it never occurred to me how odd checking in with the washing machine must have looked. There we were standing in the large atrium at the front of the building, essentially an alien environment in the context of me, myself and the washing machine, in addition to 20 suitcases. I wasn't training on the Dunmore Road anymore with just the curious neighbours for company. We were all kitted out in our Omnivend* jackets, kindly supplied by John Dowd; the uniforms made us look as if we were a visiting sports team so in addition to the washing machine we weren't difficult to miss. An initial trickle of curious onlookers turned into a steady stream of attention, and a further wave of goodwill soon washed over us. Belfast had embraced both the novelty and sentiment of our expedition.

Back home, our mission statement was getting wall-to-wall coverage on regional radio station Beat 102–103, thanks to the tremendous support offered to us by Chief Executive Gabrielle Cummins, whose own family had been darkened by the shadow of suicide. And to see a Beat-branded car, along with red and white balloons outside the Europa prior to departure, was another wonderful surprise. One of the two staff from Beat who had made the trip to Belfast, Peter Traynor, decided he would walk some of the way with me. Nine hours later, Peter arrived into Banbridge with us. Two past pupils of mine, Nicky Quinlan and Jamie Long, also turned up in Belfast before heading off 'on the tear' in Lanzarote the next day. Jamie hobbled into Banbridge with the gait of a man back on his feet following two hip replacements and both of them needed physiotherapy before they drove back to Waterford. But they'd completely embraced the spirit of the walk, and that meant so much to me. Sometimes, kindness comes along when it's least expected.

Let's rewind to that morning, Saturday, 6 June 2015. Pieta House had despatched a fine Limerick man named Johnny Togher (who has the jib of the late Irish actor and comic Niall Tóibín) across the border to wish us well on our expedition. There was a posse of print and broadcast journalists in the lobby of the Europa Hotel and a few of the reporters were happy to do some group interviews, and that suited me too. I knew there had to be a cut-off point when it came to the media and that I needed to get my food in given the enormity of the day that lay ahead. So there I was,

---

* A Waterford tech company.

starting at a buffet breakfast in the company of Maeve and my daughter, Clodagh, when Johnny sat down alongside me. I looked at Maeve, I looked at Johnny, and I knew I wasn't going to have a single sausage or slice of toasted soda bread. The enormity of what I was about to embark upon hit me right between the eyes and I began to cry. Johnny's face fell out of a smile and into a frown which to me bellowed: 'Oh Lord, we're fecked. This fella's lost it and we haven't even gotten out of the dining room.' But 10 hours later, to his evident surprise, I think Johnny felt somewhat better as I rocked up to the hotel in Banbridge with the washing machine.

Now let's rewind again 10 hours: having dried away my tears, I'd taken only two steps out of the Europa Hotel when I got a belt across the back of my head – I thought one of the lads was after giving me a slap – but it felt too strong to be friendly. It really bloody well hurt. I looked around and the harness had broken. It just snapped, and a piece of the cable had struck me. 'Jesus Christ', I grumbled to myself. 'This is not the start I had in mind.' Ann Sinnott, a scout leader who walked with us as our guide and navigator on the trip, had to go into a shop within a minute of us setting off to get directions. Mother of God, could this get any worse? Well, yes, sadly.

Towards the end of that day of unforgiving heat as we neared Banbridge (none of the wet gear we'd bought in advance would be used during any stage of the walk), I went into hypoglycaemic shock. I had had a mini-tremor, seizure, call it what you will, and I just lost it. This outdid even my worse training experience. Right then, I'd have happily taken the harness severing my shoulder as opposed to what I'd been reduced to by then. I'd taken in too much sugar, had to stop and ended up becoming very, very ill. I felt like total and utter shit (more on this anon) – and was talking it too, apparently. And when I removed the washing machine from my back that night, then and only then did it occur to me that carrying a machine emblazoned with an image of the Catholic Virgin Mary (the symbol of Pieta House) through Protestant East Belfast may not have been one of my wiser life choices! We actually passed by the front door of an Orange Order lodge before leaving the city limits and alongside the door the gospel displayed that day stated: 'The Lord has great things destined for you on this day.' That made me chuckle.

Ten miles from 'home' that first night, Kate, one of the women walking with us, said she wanted to talk to me – she'd lost a friend to suicide only a few weeks previously. She had almost decided not to join the walk, she told me. She had gone to the grave of her friend to leave some flowers there before she thought about things a bit more, opting to get on the bus with us to Belfast, and she told me how her friend died. It was powerful, difficult stuff. Talking to her that evening, I took my eye off the ball: I hadn't taken in any fluid for roughly an hour and I'd also stopped eating. Not good. Not good at all.

And now back to going 'hypo'. When I got to the hotel room and came out of the shower, I attempted to put on a pair of blue shorts. You might as well have asked me to finish a Rubik's Cube blindfolded such was the engineering quandary I found myself facing into at that moment. Clear lines felt decidedly blurry at that moment. However, I eventually got the shorts on, headed down to a double room where the massage tables had been laid out for us all, but I've precious little memory of the 90 minutes that followed. Apparently, I sat down in a chair and started shaking from top to toe: I was out of sugar and out of food. Des O'Meara (of O'Meara Brazil Physiotherapy), who has seen it all in his work with the Wexford senior footballers and countless other teams, put some sugar under my tongue, got the thermal blankets out and wrapped me up like a baby. He reassured everybody that I'd be fine and within a few minutes I can recall Maeve asking me if I was okay. My jaw was locked into position and I grunted a reply to her once I got back into my bed. I got a real jolt that night as I realised if this happened again, it was going to be a very short week, for me anyway.

The efforts extolled by a whole host of people when it came to guiding me through each of those eight days safely really went above and beyond: to me, it demonstrated the best that my adopted city has to offer: compassion, kindness and, when required, arid wit. During each day of the walk, Des O'Meara drove from Waterford city to our end of day destination just to make sure that we were looked after. We had physio and ice every day at the hotels we stayed at thanks to Des. He was there - another physio called Anthony Flanagan also offered on-site support that week - they both knew what to do and they looked after me so incredibly well, especially when I was in such difficulty that first night.

Day two, from Banbridge to Dundalk, was, literally, a pain: 10 hours of total discomfort. I remember talking to my co-writer on the home stretch into Waterford, just beyond Mullinavat in south Kilkenny - a blazing hot Sunday - and I could recall hallucinating out on the road during that second day. At least I thought it was the road, because I spent hours believing I was walking on top of a giant cobra, its head craning up in front of me in the distance. It remains a jarring sensation. Everything was spinning and I was completely gone. I had to take off the washing machine and, on advice, lie down on the road. When I eventually returned to a standing position, there was a sweaty silhouette where I'd been lying, and after a brief spell in the back of the support van, having got some fluids into the system, the cobra thankfully evaporated. Dundalk beckoned.

The lads insisted that I still had to attempt to intake some solid food so we pulled into a shopping centre in Dundalk and Daire Grant, a fire fighter, a paramedic and a great friend - he's also a qualified psychotherapist - told me straight that I just had to eat something. So we headed into the shopping centre and, this sounds like something out of a movie script, but the two of us exploded with laughter when we noted the name of the shopping centre: The Long Walk. You couldn't make it up! So in we went, standing at the deli counter, and, to my complete surprise, I lost total control of my bowels in the shop, something which had never happened to me before, and that left me having to make a hasty retreat.

And to think that the princely sum of €2 could have bunched the entire endeavour. In the final days of training, I noticed that one of the heels on my boots was starting to wear quite badly so I went to a cobbler, who had an identical match for the rubber on the boot and he changed the worn heel. But less than three days in, I was left counting the cost of that €2 outlay and that's where the real trouble started, having invested over half a year into this eight-day bloc. The skin on both my heels had come completely away by then, and my soles were pink and puce with rawness. Most of my toenails had given way by then and, come the third day, my gastric system shut down and I developed diarrhoea. Every fibre of my being - brain, arse and heels - was being put to the test. But I was desperate to stay the course, and while the road ahead remained dauntingly lengthy, I knew I had to remain headstrong.

6

Belfast to Waterford – Part Two

The blisters almost did it for me, my arse was in shreds, but the physical pounding I was subjecting myself to was far from the only pitfall that could have thrown me off course that week.

I was logging onto our Facebook page each and every night, and the messages from people who were suicidal or self-harming just kept on coming and I did my best to reply to them all, to advise them, to redirect them to services and so on. In hindsight, that was a bad call. The mental effort of processing it all really got to me. A lot of people were closely following what I was attempting to do, yet at the same time they were deeply suffering. And reading and replying to these messages brought me back to my tears and self-doubt in the Europa Hotel. It brought me back to 'The Bear'.

For a year leading up to this challenge, I'd been telling anyone willing to listen about my 'bear in a cave' analogy. The bear (i.e. the walk) was going to get one hell of a beating. I was going to humiliate him in that cave, kill him and then skin him for slippers and a coat. I was hell-bent on destroying this bear. But words are cheap. Because at the start of the walk, I was the one standing very deeply in the cave, while standing tall at the mouth of the cave, facing inwards, was the bear, who grumbled: 'You're going to do what to me?' I knew it was time to front up as these thoughts ran through my head, but that night in Dundalk, with Maeve soundly asleep, I was very, very upset. I was in the bathroom, and my feet were swollen and bleeding and I knew I was in real trouble. 'Feck,' I said to myself. 'This is not going to end well.' I was exhausted but I couldn't sleep, a horrible combination. But the following morning, the trip to the chiropodist really did the trick. Sure, I'd ended up shedding a few layers of skin off the soles of both feet, but the lancing greatly lessened my discomfort and I now knew how to dress my feet and clean them. And in my mind's eye, I found myself back in the cave, only this time the bear was nowhere to be seen. Maybe he'd embarked on a long walk of his own, but either way he was gone; I was glad to see the back of him and I was intent on keeping it that way. My worst fears could not determine my reality. After all, I was the captain of my soul. I had to keep going. And I did.

The unending hills around Drogheda and Dundalk proved major obstacles to negotiate. There was barely a strip of flat ground to walk on – but all in all, this section of the walk proved remarkably unremarkable. My body was standing up pretty well to the challenge even if the darkness I'd felt since that night in Dundalk didn't really begin to shift until we reached a small primary school in Lusk in north Dublin. By then, news of our walk had been reported extensively on radio and online and the mood was definitely improving. The light truly got back in. A teacher who had driven past us earlier got her entire primary school to come out and sing for us, and that was more powerful than any painkiller I'd taken up to that point. That sensation, coupled with catching sight of the Applegreen service station I'd stopped in with Maeve and Clodagh on the drive to Belfast only three days previously, was a source of great solace. To me it was magical, lifting the spirits in a manner similar to seeing that first sign for Dublin. It really felt like we were making progress.

Now a couple of hours further down the road, in searing heat, with a decent beard beginning to thatch over the jaw line, I found myself in a spot of physical bother and had to take a break. Eoin Keane had been intently looking at my beard before a halt was drawn. He contacted the support van via walkie talkie, asking it to wheel up alongside me. He'd noticed salt crystals on my beard, which indicated dehydration – talk about the small details making a difference; had Eoin not been paying such meticulous attention to me I could have fallen ill. Very ill. He asked the van crew for a couple of bags of crisps and then warned me not to eat them – all I could do was lick them and drop them back into both packets – and he got some liquid into me, which probably made all the difference that day. Eoin's attentiveness and duty of care had literally kept me on the road.

At our next designated break at a petrol station, we were sitting down, having a chicken sandwich and a Lucozade (it might as well have been a four-course meal), and a marvellous band called Scoops Music, featuring Stephens Cooper and O'Rourke, turned up. And while we sat there, they put on a concert; they played the drums on the washing machine and they walked for the whole day with us after that. That was so typical of the adventure that week; it brought out the best in so many people. And that goodwill fuelled me.

Liam Maher, a past pupil and member of the group who had driven ahead of us that day, nipped into Malahide and found the Irish soccer team's training base – they were in camp ahead of the Euro 2016 qualifier against Scotland the following Saturday – and he'd managed to reach out to John O'Shea, a past pupil of mine. Knowing where we were and what we were doing, John messaged us to ask would we mind if himself and a few of his friends came down to meet us – fellow international squad members at the time, including Leon Best. John handed me an Ireland jersey he'd worn to auction for charity and his first words to me were, 'Hello Mr O'Doherty' – I was still a Mister in the eyes of a Champions League winner and DLS alumnus. 'Ah John, please don't call me that,' because everyone within earshot got a giggle out of this. 'I'm sorry, sir,' replied John, to which I said, 'Come on, John, you'll have to say Enda,' to which John said, 'I can't!' Here was John, the captain of the Ireland team, one of our most heavily decorated professional footballers, and he still saw me as his teacher! We chatted for a few minutes, recorded a video for the Facebook page and then we did a spot of busking. John's humility shone brightly that day, a quality all of his De La Salle teachers had identified and admired just a few weeks after he crossed the school's threshold for the first time, aged 12.

Not long after that, Joan Freeman tracked us down. She had arranged for a fleet of cars to bring in and around 20 of us across Dublin to visit the first Pieta House in Lucan and it was a lovely moment for me as both my parents were with us by then. Joan brought us into the treatment room there and explained what happens when someone comes in seeking help. Now it just so happened that our visit coincided with someone who had made an appointment to access the service, so we had to make ourselves scarce immediately. It was the quickest I had moved that entire week!

I ended up in a walk-in cupboard off the kitchen, along with my parents and Joan Freeman, and we were told not to speak until the person went into the treatment room. And it really focused my mind: this was why we were doing this, to raise funds to help people in difficulty back home in Waterford. Once the appointment had been completed, we re-emerged from the cupboard and Joan told us about her dream: to have a Pieta

House presence throughout Ireland. And she told her story with great enthusiasm, eloquence and passion. I looked around the room as Joan spoke and saw each and every person around me touched to the core by what she'd told us: it was a special moment.

After being bussed out of the city – it was too complicated to get by foot from Lucan to where we needed to get on our southerly trek – with the rubbernecking from motorists by then reaching epidemic levels, the walk into Naas was brilliant. I saw my brother, Karl, and his two sons waiting to greet us and that was absolutely magical. There were so many memories on that road into Naas. I walked past both my primary and secondary schools and a former De La Salle colleague of mine, Peadar Hanratty (a Kildare native), came out and walked with me. We walked past a primary school where his sister worked and she had arranged for the pupils to come out to sing and wish us well. The weather was good. The company was even better. I was in absolute bits but life still felt great. The task felt utterly necessary.

From there, we advanced to Newbridge, where Rose O'Loughlin and her son Joe provided a fantastic welcome at the Keadeen Hotel. My 21st, wedding and graduation celebrations were held there, as was my sister's graduation, my son's 21st and his graduation – it's a place loaded with lovely memories. That night, my parents and the O'Loughlins joined us for dinner and it was a joy to be on home turf, followed by my best night's sleep of the entire endeavour. I woke up the following morning ready to rock, and the craic, messing and laughter the group had maintained for the entire adventure was really sustaining me. The bear wasn't even a mirage by then. He'd been banished and that felt incredibly good as we walked from Newbridge to Carlow the following day. I maintained the 'game face' while being interviewed on air daily by Beat 102–103's Andy McCloskey and even if I was visibly showing wear and tear, listeners could only hear the sunniest disposition I could muster every evening at 5.30 p.m. when Andy called. I had to remind myself about the person who might be listening to the programme, wracked and worn out by suicidal ideation. I had to remind myself of the responsibility that came with advocating for Pieta House.

By the time we reached Carlow, the jadedness coursing through my body while the washing machine was taken off my back was unlike anything I'd ever experienced up to that point in my life, let alone that week. Fergal Browne, the chairman of Carlow County Council, along with the town's Darkness into Light committee and a few more politicians, was there to greet us into the town. After the washing machine had been unloaded, I dropped to my hands and knees, not to kiss the Carlow soil or anything like that – I was completely spent and I must have been on all fours for at least 10 minutes. As I dry retched, literally willing a vomit out of my system that ultimately failed to emerge, I'd never felt so depleted in my life. I was having trouble seeing, my eyes were bloodshot with stinging sweat and the cramps running through my back and legs were contorting my entire body. I knew the welcoming party were important people because as I crouched there in ill genuflection I managed to glimpse through the vinegary sweat in my eyes to note the quality of their shoes. I briefly thought about going to dinner with Maeve, both of us in our evening best, utterly removed from skin-peeling pain, involuntary bowel movements and serpent-themed hallucinations. I eventually got to my feet, and saw beyond those gleaming black shoes to acknowledge the welcoming party as best I could and pose for photos. The smile that broke across my face did little to belie the pain I was in, but smile I did. It went with the territory.

The following morning, Fergal came our way again to officially wish us well as we made for Kilkenny, and he was so taken by our efforts that he took the day off work and walked all the way to Kilkenny with us. And there were so many other fantastic people who warmed to what we did within a matter of minutes, scrubbed their immediate plans and got walking for a mile, which inevitably turned into 10, 20 or even longer. We were all literally members of a movement, and that in itself was one hell of a reward. The kindness of strangers was made manifest to me that week, as new friendships were made while longer-standing connections were elevated.

En route to Kilkenny, I was joined on the road by Martin Molloy, probably my closest friend. His family had also come along and the walking compliment was growing bigger and bigger the closer we got to Waterford. At one stage, so he later informed me given how foggy my own memory of the week remains when it comes to certain patches, I told Martin I needed to pee. He pointed towards a gate and suggested I take off the machine and relieve myself over there, but I decided I'd hold on. We dropped back to the end of the group and, sure enough, we were approaching another gate and he suggested I go for a wee but again I said I wouldn't stop. 'I thought you said you were bursting,' he said, mildly exasperated. I replied: 'I am, but the pain from holding onto this is actually taking my mind off the pain in my feet. So when I do pee, the euphoria will be orgasmic!' Months later, Martin said by that stage of the walk I was clearly operating in a parallel universe if I was planning my pee within pleasure and pain parameters! A Garda car appeared as we neared Kilkenny to welcome us into the city for that rarest of occasions: Waterford people stopping traffic in the Cats' backyard!

A guard of honour awaited as we walked into the hotel and the mood by then was positively euphoric. The end was finally in sight. We'd seen 'WATERFORD' printed on a road sign for the very first time – it stopped us all in our tracks for photographic purposes – and that was another special moment. This was Dorothy approaching Oz levels of joy. Sure, I was in pain that night and I was upset but I knew in some way, shape or form I was going to be back home in my own bed the following night.

The following morning, as I slowly emerged from bed and gingerly trudged downstairs for breakfast, I felt the sensation of many sets of eyes trained on me as I entered the dining room. I didn't realise it right at that particular moment, but it turned out that practically everyone already having their breakfast would be walking with us to Waterford. And when I came out of the hotel, ready for the final off, there were at least 100 people kitted out for the walk, with past pupils from De La Salle among them, along with our former principal, the late Frank O'Callaghan. A kind soul named Olive Ruane, resplendent in her designer gear, dripping in gold, appeared before me – it was the first time in my life I had met Olive and she would ultimately board a flight with me to Addis Ababa two years later – and she took on that walk as if it were only a couple of miles. And that part of the walk was just terrific.

Fifteen miles from the finish, I was hauled into the van, fed and given a wash. I was told that the timeout in the van was essential given that, as more than a few of the lads put it to me, it had to be me crossing Rice Bridge with the washing machine on my back and no one else. But once I was fed and cleaned up, out I got again, and back onto my back went the machine. As we walked through Mullinavat, the Rescue 117 search and rescue helicopter passed over us and my heart sank. I turned to someone, I'm not quite sure who, and said, 'I don't want to walk into the city. When that helicopter is out, where we live that means there's someone in the river.' Most of the lads around me started laughing and told me I hadn't a clue: well, of course I hadn't a clue, I'd just spent the past week with a washing machine on my back! One of them explained: 'That's a guard of honour for you!' And at that point it really hit me. Jesus, we've walked from one end of the island to the other! The closer we got to Waterford, the more and more people were joining the walk, and other people emerged from their porches, congratulating us. And it really was a wonderful feeling. It got even better further down the road.

To my delight and surprise, there he was, standing in front me, all the way back from Canada to welcome us home: my son Oisín. What a thrill! Maeve, delirious with exhaustion, was still standing, still walking and still supporting me. The sun was beating down as we reached Sallypark, just outside the city. As a family, we huddled beneath the 'Welcome to Waterford' sign (which I also kissed) as the growing crowd of walkers and well-wishers applauded, and life, right then, in spite of the indescribable fatigue levels, never felt better. To walk into the city with my other son, Fionn (aged 10), holding my hand was beyond special. Our daughter, Clodagh, had walked from Belfast to Dublin with us. We'd all done our bit and I had never been prouder of our clan. Team O'Doherty had never stood taller.

The front line of walkers crossed Rice Bridge hand in hand, and we happily walked the length of The Quay before the great adventure finally came to an end at the Plaza, opposite Reginald's Tower. The numbers who turned out to welcome us home are still hard to quantify or fully appreciate, even with the benefit of time to reflect upon one of the greatest moments of my life. But there I was, me and my washing machine, eight days on from the tears and apprehension of a Belfast morning, back home in Waterford. We'd done it. Under the Plaza canopy I stood alongside the washing machine and spoke into a microphone, to thank everyone who had made this possible; I said everything I wanted to say – it was probably the most coherent I'd been all week within earshot of a mic! I said what was in my heart, and it all came out just right. I told my co-writer, who had walked with us from Mullinavat:

> 'I'm looking forward to going back to being an ordinary Joe Soap, standing in a chipper. I'm looking forward to Paddy Power's – I miss my gambling – and I'm looking forward to going to France with my wife and my children, making sandcastles, relaxing and just getting back to normality. There's a lot to be said for normality.'

As I hobbled away from the Plaza, alongside Maeve and the kids, and back towards the comfort of home that balmy Sunday evening, despite my raw heels, despite experiencing the most profound tiredness of life, two words ran through my mind over and over and over. What's next?

7

Teacher Man

Truth be told: I accidentally ended up in teaching. I sat my Leaving Certificate in 1986 and back then if you had a set of Crayola that was enough to get you into a degree level course. Want proof? Look no further than this washing machine carrier! I went to Maynooth because my sister was studying there and for no other reason, taking a degree in Ancient Greek and Roman Civilisations. After all, I'd taken Latin in secondary school, seen at least part of a Ray Harryhausen movie and firmly believed without any real authority that the Romans had a good thing going for a while. Let's not forget sanitation, medicine, education, wine, public order, irrigation, roads, the freshwater system, and public health. Now I'm pretty sure someone else thought of these accomplishments long before I did. In fact, the same folk told us to 'always look on the bright side of life' so I probably owe Monty Python a great deal more than I ever realised before I considered what lay beyond the end of my nose, personally, academically or professionally.

I also took Modern Irish Literature through Irish (why opt for a standardised bar after all?), Psychology and Geography. Talk about eclectic! I reached the end of my studies without any firm idea about what lay ahead of me, but my mother knew what the time demanded: 'You'd better go and do that H.Dip. so you'll at least be qualified for something,' she suggested. Given that my only qualification by that time was an uncanny ability to get utterly sozzled, I took on board my mother's advice and by God that was one good decision. So I got H-Dipped and became a

Geography teacher. And from day one, teaching and I made for a fully consensual fit.

I'd never been the musical or dramatic type, but standing at the top of a classroom felt like my calling right from the off. I'm effectively on stage at De La Salle College for four hours a day, and I've got a captive if not always captivated audience – it's not like they can leave! If you just come in and read out of a book or write notes on a board, then you're on a one-way ticket to Drudgeville. But if you come in enthused, engaged and energetic some of that buzz will generally resonate with a quorum of students, and they'll respect you for that, and that's what I've devoted most of my professional energy to since I stopped drinking. I enjoy the fun of teaching: when you see most faces in a classroom wondering what the hell is going on with 'your man' behind the desk as they laugh hysterically at times, it's hard not to get pleasantly swept along with that. Contrary to the stereotype, school can, at times, be enjoyable. There's space for that in the curriculum. You just have to read between the lines is all. It can be done and I love the magic of it.

I can vividly remember my first staff meeting at De La Salle College in 1990. A 40-minute debate ensued about whether or not white socks should be permissible as part of the school uniform: Michael Jackson was sporting them gig in, gig out as he toured the world at the time, so, yes, back then at De La Salle it did indeed matter if your socks were black or white.

Two other teachers had also just joined the staff and, as newbies tend to do, we sat together at the meeting, quietly minding our own business, while energetically nodding on occasion, just as TV news reporters do for cutaway shots during interviews. I turned to them both and quietly queried: 'Did we really spend four years in university for discussions like this?' We grinned equally quietly while continuing to nod and wink. This was it. The real world, and I was now a tax-paying unionised member of it. Christ. 1990. It's as if someone clicked their fingers and here I am, a generation later, and, blessedly, I'm still here. Teaching but no longer merely surviving. A lot has changed in my life in that time, but through it all, my relationship with De La Salle has remained a constant, and I'm glad of it. And even at the apex of my drinking, I was never out of work. I was never even late, come to think of it.

Despite that, there were times during my own 'Lost Weekend' when, a little like Osama bin Laden in Abbottabad, I was hiding in plain sight. I remember one teacher, during his retirement address, declaring how much he'd miss 'Enda, sitting in the corner of the staff room, eating a breakfast roll while holding a bottle of Lucozade'. 'Feck,' I said to myself as his words bore into me, like cold water running down my back. In those days, I required an obscene amount of sugar, caffeine and fat to kickstart the engine after whatever I'd poisoned myself with the previous night. When I tell people at a presentation that I'm an alcoholic, I regularly get the feeling that a few people sharing that space with me imagine me holed out under a bridge, hunkered into a cardboard box, with just a mangy dog, a half-empty brandy bottle and bittersweet memories for company.

Yet sometimes, being in plain sight is the safest place to be for an addict. Whenever we had a staff outing, I presented the illusion that I was healthy and safe by not bringing the car – I used to walk to 'the do'. The chances were that I would have already downed a half bottle of vodka en route, which I 'cleverly' concealed inside a soft drink bottle. And to think people would admire me for leaving the car at home; by the time I'd reach the bar I was already half shot thanks to one shot too many. There were nights I would have knocked back 20 pints and congratulated myself for it. I saluted myself for my own gross denial – and I did that for years. Some hero, drinking pints of vodka at least twice a week, but still functioning. Still teaching.

Nicola Lee is an art teacher at De La Salle and she's been a valued colleague and friend for many years. We've seen both our families grow up together, and when I rid myself of alcohol I also realised I had to bin the dishonesty and deceit that had been a trademark of my drinking. So once I grabbed my ticket to board the good ship Sobriety, I had to come clean with Nicola. I told her: 'Nicky, I was never in your house – ever – without drinking a full bottle of spirits from your cabinet.' She could not believe it. I had done this deed repeatedly with such stealth and finesse that she'd never once noticed what I did and how I did it. But here's the thing: I was having a good time through it all. Mindless drinking did not mean misery for me. It became part of my life, just like teaching. But I get so much more out of teaching now in my sobriety. Kicking booze to touch has made life better in every way.

Teaching's a hard job: I've lost count of how often that motion has been tabled in my company. Really? It's an absolutely brilliant job. I work 167 days each year and have a 22-hour week. Even in the days when I reckon I'd have given Brendan Behan a run for his money at a bar counter, I've never considered it in those terms. Once I enter the busy corridors of De La Salle, be it first thing in the morning or between classes, absolutely anything can happen and I love the element of surprise. Of course, there's the 'pull the chord' side of work which kicks in once you've the miles built up, a little like reciting the Nicene Creed at Mass: you say the words from childhood and eventually deliver them without dwelling for too long on what it is you're actually saying. For example, when it comes to, say, a v-shaped valley for Leaving Cert Physical Geography (80 marks), you're talking about two pages of exam writing, with 15 minutes allocated to each page. Such a lesson typically kicks off like this:

> 'A v-shaped valley is found in the upper course of a river. The v shape has been made by hydraulic action, abrasion and solution: hydraulic action - the physical force of the water; abrasion - the wearing of the river against the bed; solution - chemical alteration occurs, linking hydration, oxidation, and carbonation...'

So while there's some auto-piloted stuff at play annually, the really good teachers strive to learn more than they teach - at least that's how I see it. My OCD dictates that each October or November, I'll begin to work on my end-of-year comments for the Sixth Year students. I always strive for something meaningful in such a salutation, even if I privately concede that an 'Oh Captain, My Captain' moment is probably not on the cards when these energetic, bright young men cross the threshold of my classroom one last time. Striving to make a positive impression with your students is something worth pursuing, and that ambition sustains me in the day job - it encourages me to do better and demand more of myself.

Of course, teachers aren't popularity seekers - at least they shouldn't be - but let's face it: a day in the classroom is made a lot easier for everyone sharing such a space when there's at least a tolerable level of accord. That tends to build mutual respect, and that in turn greatly enhances the prospect of getting some good work done on any given school day. Anything that makes life easier ought to be pursued. One of the greatest privileges I've had as a teacher is the knowledge I've acquired from so many students. They have taught me so much, coming from a wide variety of backgrounds, socioeconomic groups and, increasingly so in recent years, races. I've been enriched by their curiosity, warmth and good humour. And I hope they've elicited some benefit from both my teaching and, when it's been sought out individually, my counsel. And my being the 'washing machine man' has helped.

Since the Belfast to Waterford walk, I've had at least ten students knocking on my door, telling me that they feel like they've run out of options, that it was me or the river. Their question is as profound as any

I've ever faced: 'Mr O'Doherty, what will I do?' That they've felt comfortable enough in their relationship with me to take that step and make that admission really is something. One of these lads told me he'd been struggling badly for six months, so he sat with me, hoping my words could help him to find a way out of a cul-de-sac with 60-feet-high walls on either side and little, if any, light getting in. He was in a state of deep panic yet he still felt he could confide in me. 'The reason you feel like you're dying,' I told him, 'is that the primeval part of your psyche is telling you that a dinosaur is going to separate your head from your body. There is no dinosaur. No dinosaur.' And as we sat, and as he listened, I could see some of the tension easing as I told him about what had happened to me before suggesting what to do were I in his shoes. And to see a kid emerge from that fog of crippling uncertainty, having sought help, having opted to share the load, is incredible.

That knock on the door does cause me some level of upset because I can realise, in my own mind, what that kid is feeling. And when you talk to a parent and hear the anguish in their voice over what's going to happen to their child, and how helpless they feel about their son's suffering, those are tough and difficult conversations to have. But they're utterly necessary: a few of them may well have saved a young life struggling with studies, a relationship breaking down, substance abuse or agonising over matters of sexuality. If a kid tells me he's not feeling well I go through a checklist, and when I share it with a student they generally look at me somewhat in awe, trying to figure out how I'd figured out what was going on in their own confused and windswept mindset. Once I tell them what they're feeling is quite common you can feel some of that tension lifting, but, at the same time, a lot of these exchanges can get very close to the bone, and it can be tough to leave that sentiment behind you once the sun sets on another school day.

Sadly, during my time at De La Salle three students have taken their lives by suicide. I knew one of them through soccer but never taught any of them. Would I have made any difference in any of their lives had I been a teacher of theirs? I've no idea. To claim I could have made a difference would be the height of arrogance as we've got great teachers right across this school, all doing their utmost day in, day out to help students both holistically and academically. But one of the events that spurred me into fundraising and campaigning was attending the funeral of the student I had known through sport at St Mary's Church in Ballygunner. There wasn't a spare seat in sight. The cries of his mother filled the church. Her upset was as total as it was horrific. Every parent's worst nightmare.

The level of pain she was in genuinely shocked me. I left that church wondering was there something I could do in some way to impact positively upon families in Waterford so that other parents could be spared that devastated woman's agony. It was a major trigger for me. It spurred me into action. It helped to somewhat re-frame my sobriety. I felt I had to put this new-found clarity to better use.

Nowadays, if I meet a past pupil whom I had responsibility for between 1990 and 1995, the first thing I do is apologise: in those days, I patrolled my classroom like an SS commandant. It was my way of surviving when I was still in my early 20s. I used to live directly across from the school and every day at either breaktime or lunchtime, I used to nip back to the house to change my shirt given how soaked my initial garment was from perspiration. If a lad in my class hadn't his homework done, I would shout at the guilty party and retain that volume for the following 40 minutes. I don't think I've raised my voice in a classroom for over three years at this stage: what was par for the course is now a special event! And in this particular guise, the discipline levels in my classroom have never been better – hardly a coincidence, methinks. The kids respect the fact that I respect them and that says something for the journey I've taken in my sobriety. I'm a different person and that's down to what I've learned about myself. It's allowed me to progress on all levels.

If you're still teaching the same way in your late 40s the way you did in your early 20s, for me, there's something wrong. Sometimes I look back at all those horrible days and wished they'd never happened, but those days are a part of who I was, and the lessons learned from those experiences have made me who I am today. And when I do have rough patches, which I still do from time to time, the difference today is that I'm aware of how I feel while also recognising what I need to do to get through such phases. Living has shown me that there is always an alternative, and that's one of the benefits that comes from age: identifying a problem without allowing it to rule you. Youngsters don't always have that capacity. So when a student wants to share a problem with me, the message I attempted to convey when carrying the washing machine gains value. I know I've done some good at some level, and that's an incredible feeling. And I've allowed myself to feel good about that.

In a teaching career, there are innumerable times when a student steps out of line: of course, there's no doubt that a student would proffer the same standpoint, albeit from an opposing perspective. But one incident springs to mind in which I can recall a student who was completely and utterly wrong. Now I could have come down on him like a ton of pissed-off teachers trapped beneath a ton of bricks: the parents could have been called for, detention and suspension could well have followed, but the bigger goal here was to change this lad's behaviour. I needed him to stop doing what he'd been doing for some time, so I opted for something different instead: an underused but easily availed of human commodity – kindness. It's quite bizarre how some people just cannot cope with positivity: the last thing they expect to receive as part of the path of least resistance is oddly more difficult for the 'out-of-liner' to process than a smorgasbord of punishments. After all, most people don't tune into *Liveline* expecting Joe Public to colonise Joe Duffy's headphones with saccharine-scented tales of unbridled joy.

Anyway, when this particular student came in for his meeting with me, he'd clearly told himself beforehand that he was in for it now, and that all manner of hellfire was about to be unleashed upon him. I looked at him, he looked at me and I began by putting it to him: 'How did Liverpool give away a three-goal lead last night?'

'Wha,' he muttered, unable to fully enunciate a teenager's favourite four-letter word, while nearly falling off his chair given the levity of my question. And for the next 15 minutes we spoke about soccer; he'd stopped shifting awkwardly in his seat and actually appeared to be enjoying the conversation. And then we got to talking about some positives.

'Well, one of the good things about this chat so far is that you haven't sworn yet,' I put it to him sunnily. 'And you haven't shown any signs of wanting to take a swing at me, which is even better! But what you and I need to do now is to come up with a plan so that you and I don't have to have a chat like this again because I need to keep you out of the principal's office, because once you're in there I can't help you.' And that approach worked; he settled into school and everything has been fine for him ever since. And there's as much satisfaction for me in helping to resolve an issue for a student like that as there is in seeing each and every student delivering as best they can in academic terms.

I remember another student approaching me one day in school for a note to sign out. He was in Sixth Year and his entire school experience, from my perspective, was all about blending in. He'd never missed a day, he'd never been late, he'd never been in any trouble and he'd never failed a test. He cruised through school. When people think about the Manchester United team that won the Champions League, Premier League and FA Cup in 1999, you'd be hard pressed to meet too many supporters or non-fans who would pick out Nicky Butt as a key performer in that remarkable season. But anyone who played almost

400 times for United during Alex Ferguson's reign and was described as 'a fantastic servant' by his 'gaffer' clearly had a lot going for him. Butt was part of the spine of that group's effort and his worth has been widely hailed by those he soldiered with without being championed too widely beyond Old Trafford. Society is largely composed of people like that student who just got on with things during his six years with us, someone who probably couldn't readily see just how well he had done throughout his time in De La Salle, without ever having his name up in lights. He's indicative of most of society: good people who just get on with their lives, people who don't seek or cause drama, winning without ever realising the extent of their own triumph.

The greater triumph for a lot of teenagers isn't contained within the slip of paper containing their Leaving Certificate results: it's in simply surviving those years between childhood and college. There's so much learning in those years that teachers are not primarily responsible for, be it in coping with your first heartache, dealing with difficulties at home, coming to terms with one's sexuality, etc. We might be able to touch on those issues in various guises, but the meat and potatoes of them are resolved away from the classroom. And in an age when a plethora of television shows beam images of dazzling straight teeth and perfect bodies (tanned of course), all occupying environments in which nobody appears to work, crisis management can be problematic. In fact, some teenagers have no coping skills whatsoever. When things go south, they simply don't know what to do. They haven't clocked up enough mileage to know what needs to be done when a fire starts to gain more and more oxygen – they don't know how to put it out.

So when we teachers have an opportunity to, at the very least, assist in resolving an issue for a student, as I've regularly experienced when it comes to indiscipline, the real triumph from my perspective is when you never end up having the 'big chat' after that initial face-to-face meeting. There's enormous satisfaction when you feel you've got through to someone, and you're not likely to receive that without gaining a student's respect. The same logic applies with those colleagues you share a staff room with: you can't expect to be bosom buddies with everyone traversing in and out of 'Grand Central', grabbing a quick cuppa before embarking on whatever train line makes up their daily tour of this imposing slab of Waterford plaster and woodchip. But you can at least try and offer respect: do that and the chances are you'll get it in return. Life, be it at work or at home, is a lot easier when respect is in orbit. And when you consider that some students nicknamed me 'Satan' during my drinking years, I think it's fair to say I'm neither the same man nor teacher that I was back in that goatee-wearing phase of mine. After all, it's not just the students who have to busy themselves with learning and growing day in, day out. And that pleases me. That's what drives me on.

8

Building the Machine

When I listen to music, I 'hear' colours. I remember when I first pointed this out to Maeve her response was: 'Stop making things up to make yourself sound odd. You're odd enough already!'

But it's true. I hear a certain genre and I sense a colour. I've had a lifelong connection to music. My mother, who was a piano teacher, was offered a place in the RTÉ Symphony Orchestra, so I grew up in a house where music was more frequently heard than a singing kettle on the range, and it's been with me ever since. When I'm on my way home from a Leinster match or coming back from a seminar, I'll listen to some Chopin or Schubert. Before I go on stage, I'll have dance music funnelled into my headphones. Going into the gym, I'll have music to wind me up, and, following a workout, I'll have music that winds me down. I've never, ever exercised in my life without music, nor with all the reds, oranges and yellows that tend to go with it. And if the music matches my mind, it actually benefits the quality of my exercise session. Not having any control over the music is one of the things I don't like about going to public classes with an instructor and I regularly find myself not trying as hard as I do within my own musically-controlled exercise environ-ment. Cut me some slack here: my addictive personality manifests itself in many different ways nowadays, none of which send me off a high board and into the bottom of a bottle, thankfully.

As well as sensing a colour while the sweat streams onto the gym floor beneath me, I tend to exercise in imagination. Two minutes into a session, while I am physically in the gym, my mind has shot through the ceiling above me like a Saturn rocket escaping Earth's gravity. When preparing for Belfast to Waterford, just a matter of moments into those first gym sessions, I'd be teleported 20 miles outside Dundalk to such an extent that the other people and sounds around me dissolved. Visualisation is a powerful tool and for months prior to being actually out on the road and in the middle of its heel-slicing, bowel-emptying, hallucinogenic reality, I'd close my eyes and I was on that road. It might have been eight days of real-time activity but, for me, I'd walked that route for months.

I suspect those sharing gym space with me on those early mornings must have been wondering what the hell I was at. We'd be just gearing up for a spin class at, say, 7 a.m., and I'd already be drenched in sweat having run or lifted weights for the previous half-hour, seeing red in the best possible sense before allowing myself some downtime in the subtler mauves and lilacs. When it came to pre-Kilimanjaro, I'd regularly have worn an oxygen deprivation mask, cutting the jib of a Christy Moore/ Darth Vader crossover, spinning at full pelt to the point where, to any onlooker, I'd appear odds on to either vomit or faint.

But in my mind, for however zany I must have looked to everyone else working up a less voluminous but slightly more sane level of workday sweat, I was ferrying that washing machine closer and closer to Uhuru Peak. Every drop of sweat dampening the floor beneath me was bringing me a step nearer to my goal. I visualised unfurling the tricolour at Africa's highest point and I attempted to imagine that moment of exhalation, of exhilaration, of accomplishment. And it made me work harder and harder and harder. And every single training session was like that.

But that came at a price. I tend to train too hard, and those reds and oranges I'd sense would frequently catalyse pink dots that I'd actually see. Training in top gear inevitably leads to injuries and niggles, which in turn impacts negatively on your wish to train consistently over weeks, even months. Consistent effort is what Conor McDonald extolled to me, and this was something I had to learn to strive for and adapt to: it's better to hit 75 to 80 per cent of your potential in training for a sustained period and then, as your event draws closer, take the risk of upping the workload while attempting to contain your peak for when you need it most. Having been no more than a moderately talented sportsperson, I always strove to achieve an extraordinary level of endeavour, and that was reflected in my commitment when training for both Belfast to Waterford and Kilimanjaro. But it was only when I tapped into expert coaching that I began to recognise that leaving the tap on the whole time isn't great in terms of building endurance.

I was also consumed by the fear of failure, and that served to motivate me during training. I couldn't envisage a scenario where I had to drop out somewhere between Belfast and Waterford, so the fear of not following through made me train even harder. And it got to the point where, having worked out in top gear before going to work, I would return to the gym that same evening and I'd go again, off into my own world, somewhere along the eastern seaboard, me and my washing machine. Titles are won in pre-season. That was the logic which was driving me on to increase my physical output and enhance my strength levels. I aimed for the dark spaces no one else could see, getting in those five extra push-ups, then doing five more on top of that the following morning. To lift a washing machine from one end of the country to the other, I had to reconstruct me: to build my own physical machine. I was fully committed to investing my entire being into this endeavour, both physically and mentally. Balls to the wall. All or nothing. Enda 2.0. That's who I'd become, and it's the skin I'm still happiest in.

Conor McDonald played a huge role in broadening my education when it came to building the machine. After an initial conversation, he figured out what mechanics I needed when it came to carrying the washing machine: he honed in on my traps, my deltoids, lower back, upper back and shoulders. Conor's plan was to make me robotically strong and if I was physically stronger than I needed to be through a strict range of exercises, then I stood a far less chance of physically breaking down, so that ultimately my survival on this walk would come down to what I had going on between my ears. The plan was to build a physical structure over four months in the gym that would have me ready and raring to go when I hit the road with the washing machine.

And his level of planning was meticulous. Conor's pull-ups, for example, involved being as slow as you could pull up to the bar, followed by a peel which totally unwound the body, and you'd be doing brilliantly to get through three or four of them because achieving the perfect placements of both hands and shoulders was absolute agony. Necessary agony. In Conor's world, quality supersedes quantity each and every time and, as I discovered, that included the primacy of a proper warm-up – an alien world to me prior to those sessions. I can remember being consumed by pain during one warm-up: Conor put me through shoulder flexibility exercises where I would put my arms against a wall, placing me at different angles with my hip flexors and with my quads and shoulders. It was thorough and it was what I needed. He armed me with the common sense I would marry with my own mental resilience, drawing value out of every pull-up, deadlift and farmer's lift.

Everything about the 'Modified Strongman' programme which Conor developed for me was based on quality and I'll be forever indebted to him for the expertise he shared with me over four sweat-sozzled, muscle-building months. I needed Conor's discipline and control – and it worked. From lifting the yoke, which left my neck red raw after each session, to carrying chains in the gym and powering the prowler up and down the hall (followed by work on the punchbag), he drew measured, controlled work out of me. The emphasis on technique led to visible results over those months, and thanks to Conor I took huge strides forward. Everything he tasked me to do in his gym helped to get me from one end of Ireland to the other by foot.

What might have been viewed as a fly in the preparatory ointment thankfully didn't come to pass, but again Conor factored my decades-old back issue into my programme. Taking my old rugby injury into account, how my own load-bearing would hold up to carrying a washing machine was something I obviously had to factor into my plans, and a lot of people put it to me that my back must have been in bits. But the funny thing was that my back couldn't have been better. I'd been doing back exercises and back extensions every day for several years, and the first time Conor put me into a back extension machine, where your legs are strapped in and you lean forward, I think I failed on two reps. Before we went to Kilimanjaro, I was able to do between 30 and 40 reps while holding 50 kilos. When I walk, I can feel the strength that I've developed in my lower back – and that's all down to looking after it over a prolonged period.

I believe we all have a natural, physical ability. Mine is built on endurance. I'm quite a stocky build, so I'm probably best designed for short, explosive events. In truth, I'm probably the 'wrong' shape for Ironman: I could well have achieved better results if I'd trained for the 100 or 200 metres. But, right from the off, endurance events felt like a good fit. Over the shorter distances – the sprint triathlons – I found myself falling further and further off the pace, but over the longer distances I began to improve and that was something I tapped into when preparing for Belfast to Waterford. Switching off while staying focused over long distances and several hours. Literal muscle memory. And it all helped to build my confidence. Learning how to do a handstand push-up at 45, thanks to Geina McGrath at Conor's gym, tends to help on that front. It made me feel like Superman.

Another key element in training for the Belfast to Waterford walk was the people whom I was surrounded by. The encouragement and support I received from fellow members at the Kingfisher Gym in Waterford at the time was spiritually nourishing. As word began to filter around about me and my washing machine expedition, the cause I was walking for and my reasons for taking it on began to outweigh the bizarreness of the task at hand. The human element intensified. People began to approach me in the gym to wish me well and that encouragement certainly improved my physical training. It made the training more enjoyable. And I had the same experience when preparing for Kilimanjaro in the WIT Arena gym. The support was fantastic, but so too was the kick I got in seeing the expressions of young lads, there on sports scholarships, watching someone old enough to be their father lifting weights they couldn't believe I was capable of burdening. People were drawn to why I took on these challenges, and that was genuinely uplifting. There was indeed method to my madness.

Fortunately for me, training never felt like a burden. I never missed a session in preparing for the walk, and even to myself I never said that I didn't want to train. I know feeling that way about training allowed me to do more than just tolerate what I was putting myself through. I was enjoying it. This wasn't about an alcoholic flagellating himself during sobriety. I had discovered something which I could tap into, which I could mould and develop into something, improving my mind while developing my body. There were no medals or lucrative contracts waiting for me to sign at the finish line. There was something altogether more satisfying: firstly, an opportunity to publicise the Pieta House message and, secondly, to do something which my wife and children would be proud of. Any self-satisfaction I had was somewhere well down the line after that.

Routine is a fundamental in every facet of my life so it will come as no surprise that I developed an obsessiveness about my training kit: I would have the gear out the night before, the right socks, the right underwear – if you're carrying a washing machine for eight or nine hours on a Saturday hike, you want to make sure you're got the right jocks on! I always had my gear ready and I always had a smile on my face. I was always, always, always, ready to rock. Why? Because the alternative didn't appeal to me. That mantra about doing something every day that others won't do, and one day you can achieve something that others can't, is the sort of air I like breathing in. Anything worth doing takes time and I truly invested in my time while preparing for Belfast to Waterford. This wasn't homework being assigned by the teacher. This wasn't something I had to do. I wanted to do it and that's what made it so enjoyable.

And then there's Maeve. She's been there from day one in all of this. She has seen me in all my manifestations and never been anything other than fully opted in. The Wise to my Morecambe. During the road sessions with the washing machine, it was quite tough at times to get the training in. After word began to get around about why I was taking on this challenge, it got to the stage that any time I was out people would approach me to talk about the loved ones they had lost to suicide, and more often than not such conversations were stationary: I wasn't getting anywhere physically and such exchanges - warm, heartfelt and emotional as they were - were eating into my training time. So Maeve allowed me to talk to people but, like a guardian angel, she was always there, just over my shoulder, looking out for me. And when it came to Belfast to Waterford, she applied one principle for the week: that I wasn't to stand still while anyone talked to me, and it made sense. If one person stopped me for only 10 minutes a day for six days that week, I would have lost an hour on the road. And true to my word, and adhering to the principle Maeve had suggested, any chat I had that week was conducted while moving, as the plethora of journalists I encountered that week can testify to!

Taking off the suit after school every day at 3 p.m. and hoisting on the washing machine was an odd sensation; setting off down the Dunmore Road (the most congested strip of tarmac in Waterford), with so many students and parents sat in their slowly moving cars, looking at me as I set off on a session. That took a lot of getting used to. But as time moved on, every Wednesday evening meant three hours on the road and, soon enough, a group began to come out training with me, friendships developing as the routine took root. Each Saturday and Sunday entailed lengthy, endurance-building walks of 20 to 26 miles each day, and I have to admit I never really found those walks to be all that hard because I had developed such physical strength. It was really only at the end of those walks, after the physical exertion of it, after all the jokes, the fluid intake, the eating and so on, that I'd feel spent, cognisant that everything I had done today I would have to do again tomorrow.

The routine of training created huge stability for me and served to drive me on. Yes, this involved sacrifice but the level of sacrifice involved in this process deepened my motivation. It made a physically stronger man. It made me mentally tougher and I'd like to think it made me a better person.

Of course, even the very best preparation cannot account for every eventuality. In the nine or so months training for Belfast to Waterford, I didn't have a single blister. But on day one, walking out of Belfast, I had blisters! Physically, prior to Kilimanjaro, I was considerably stronger and fitter than I had been setting off from Belfast and also had a considerably better harness on the washing machine, but altitude sickness hit me like a punch I'd never seen coming.

My dad, on more than one occasion, has been moved to remind me: 'Remember, you know nothing.' He's right. What I've learned from Conor McDonald remains with me every time I go to the gym. His advice regularly crossed my mind on those weekends I hiked the Comeragh Mountains preparing for Kilimanjaro, carrying a rucksack weighing 40 kilos while sometimes wearing an oxygen mask. But my dad's words were also up there on the mountain with me. Catching sight of the 'Welcome to Waterford' sign with my family as we neared the end of the walk from Belfast also passed through the mind's eye. Routinely reaching physical exhaustion was not a thought I had when I performed the back-stroke through alcohol, but there was a purpose to what I was doing. And conscious as I was of remaining outwardly positive to those training with me, I strove to wear a smile through it all. Whether that helped or not is for others to adjudicate on, but I could see lots of smiling people around me during training, drawing the best out of each other. I could see a team building right in front of me, and that teamwork magnificently came to pass on the slopes of Kilimanjaro. And Maeve was there, by my side, to see this materialising. And that's worth more to me now than reaching the summit. That chapter of my life still had a happy ending – and there's a few more that remain unwritten. There's got to be.

9

Summit Story – Part One

14 July 2017. When news broke back home of an Irish death on Kiliman-jaro, an understandable conclusion was reached: that we had lost one of our team. We were actually all home by then, but more than a few people had, again understandably, lost track of our timeline. My co-writer told me he'd feared the worst having heard the news from his car while driving away from Mahon Falls, high in the Comeragh Mountains, a landmark many of us had grown accustomed to taking in during our training hikes in the build-up to Kilimanjaro.

Majella Duffy, from Rathcormac in east Cork, was 35 years old. She was climbing Kilimanjaro in memory of her late father, Mike, who, aged 47, had suffered a fatal heart attack in 2001; she'd travelled to Tanzania to raise funds for the Irish Heart Foundation (IHF). Majella, only daughter to Mike and her mother, Bernie, was described in the *Irish Times* as 'a person of extraordinary drive and energy'. I suspect we would have encountered kindred spirits had our paths ever crossed.

During his homily at Majella's funeral mass, Canon Michael Leamy recalled a coffee morning held on 23 April, less than three months before the sad news emerged from an altitude of 4,000 metres. 'None of us who called that day could have envisaged what is taking place today,' he told mourners. 'All who supported the many fundraising events that Majella was involved in organising no doubt feel the same today.' Canon Leamy stated:

> 'A part of the mission of the Irish Heart Foundation is to affect positive change in the lifestyles of Irish people and to achieve better outcomes for those affected by heart disease and stroke. Majella, over the past four or five years, through her dedication to fitness, lived that mission.'[4]

Having requested that nobody from our team post anything online when the awful news initially broke – some of the lads were getting multiple calls and texts asking were they okay – come 5 p.m. that day I posted a message which confirmed that everyone was safe and home. It was, nonetheless, an utterly numbing 24 hours. It really focused the mind on just how dangerous a trek we'd taken on. It made the warmth of home all the more insulating.

I felt as if I had read a million articles, watched a million videos and bookmarked a million books about Kilimanjaro before boarding the plane. Despite that, I really didn't have a clue until I was out there, on the slopes, living it. It was as hard and difficult a thing as I could ever imagine, multiplied by five. And it was like that for everyone. It was off the scale, the best and worst times of my life all mixed up. The Belfast to Waterford effort was like a day in a crèche in comparison. Hand on heart.

And a day into the ascent, just a single day, I thought I was in 'game over' territory. Failure was staring me right in the face, and I'd barely set foot on African soil – granted, we'd completed the equivalent of four Carrauntoohils on day one – so everything is relative, I guess.

Knowing I had to eat, having left Shira Camp (3,800 metres), I sat and ate; well, I sat and I attempted to eat. It took me a full hour to eat three slices of toast, and I had to cut them into small triangles on my plate – I couldn't lift them in their uncut form, that's how banjaxed I was. There's a photograph of me with my head down on a table, alongside the plate of toast. It might as well have been concrete I was trying to ingest. That's what altitude does to you. This was jadedness taken to a whole new dimension – with a washing machine on my back for good measure.

The environment we were climbing in was utterly alien to me. Day one and the four Carrauntoohils came with 30-degree heat and 90 per cent humidity thrown in for sadistic measure. It was all uphill – the ascent featured some downhill reprieves along the way – and we finished in the dark, in a rainforest, in the rain. And by the time I got into camp that night, I was destroyed. I was astounded by how quickly things had unravelled.

I didn't sleep at all that night. Not a wink. I was on a slope, lying on rock-hard ground, and I felt terrible. Attempting to sleep at altitude is akin to having someone kneel on your chest the entire night; the rhythm I needed to get into a deep sleep had been poached from my lungs by the mountain. The following morning, Gary Freeman took the washing machine for about two hours, and then I resumed carrying duties. And about two hours into that stint, I developed a piercing headache. I closed my right eye as it eased the pain somewhat, and after a while, crazy and all as it sounds, I closed my left eye and opened my right – I couldn't keep both of them open such was the severity of the headache. Now I've had a lumbar puncture and migraines previously, but this was physical pain and irritation of an intensity I had never endured before. And then I fainted, but I didn't hit the deck, which was just as well considering the white goods I had strapped across my back. Instead, I slumped onto the hiking poles, which was – in a completely selfish sense – brilliant because the doctor hadn't noticed that I'd lost consciousness, but within a few minutes I was lying on the ground, vomiting uncontrollably. And boy, do I mean uncontrollably – think *Team America: World Police* levels. Nature was napalming my guts.

The entire scene was like a bad cartoon. There I was, Enda 2.0, Mr Motivator, the zany De La Salle teacher, and I was making an unwelcome reacquaintance with the Shira Camp toast. I managed to lift my head and look across the path towards a large boulder, where just at that moment – I kid you not – a vulture landed.

This was Monty Python material ('bring out your dead!') and I would have laughed had it not been for the globules of vomit my body was still chucking up. Louise Walsh, who spoke so powerfully in the Seanad about not being able to access mental health services for her son, was walking by as I lay there on the ground, surrounded by my own secretions, and she said whimsically, 'Are you okay, Maeve?' In my frazzled mind, I was intoning, 'well feck you, Louise, I'll get you back for that' – Irish people are so sympathetic!

I was dehydrated by day two. I was fatigued in a manner I had never before experienced and I don't know how I got back to camp that day. The lads were 'Sharing the Load' with the washing machine even earlier than I had anticipated. I realised that within a few hours of getting this unprecedented uphill show on the road, what lay ahead would prove a physical and mental examination unlike anything I'd ever put myself through. Lugging the washing machine up Slievenamon and the Comeraghs during training was one thing: but this was different gravy.

The next morning, aided by some powerful steroids, my system needed a jump lead and boy did I get it. In addition, I took nausea and headache tablets and I genuinely felt a lot better. 'I can do this' was running on a loop internally and I was determined to make the very best of this situation and to give the very best of myself. And while knowledge goes a long way, ignorance can prove just as influential on a trip like this, as I uncomfortably discovered. You see, if you take codeine at altitude, it magnifies your headache, but there I was, the stupid Paddy, downing what I considered to be a restorative mixer of paracetamol and codeine, and all I was doing was digging a hole for myself. Of course, I should have asked the doctor beforehand, and that was all on me, and the intensifying headache proved a lesson painfully learned.

We also had to try to drink at least six litres of water a day. Now, if you're at home, more or less at sea level, on the hottest of Irish days, you're not going to drink that much water, even if you're training for a marathon. But while we were on that mountain, I dropped a kilo a day. Now I can think of more pleasant ways to shed some timber as that weight loss was indicative of my body's inability to cope with altitude. I had intended to eat between 5,000 and 6,000 calories a day but in reality I was clearly taking in less than that given my weight loss. The discomfort felt unrelenting, and it wasn't just me. We collectively suffered, but the good humour and camaraderie, amidst the irritable bowels and violent vomiting, was astounding. In many ways, that spirit was the fuel that carried us onward and kept us all dreaming.

By the time we reached the bleak and rugged beauty of the Lava Tower (4,695 metres), situated between Shira Camp and the Barranco Huts, I actually felt okay again. I was at the back of the group on approach to the tower and was carrying a few bags at that point, and I felt as good as I had at any stage since the great adventure began. The headache had abated and it felt as if my brain had unswollen. 'I can do this' remained on a loop, and every step taken was a step closer to the summit, to sitting on the washing machine and unfurling my tricolour. By the time we left the Lava Tower behind us, I genuinely felt great. The human body remains the most remarkable machine ever built, and my vomiting in the company of a vulture was by then a receding memory.

From there, we entered the sheer drop of the Karanga Valley – take the steepest land drop in the Comeraghs and multiply it by five – for two to three hours and then up the other side. I was carrying the washing machine and by then I felt like Superman. Tip top. Absolutely brilliant. And I felt even better when I slowed my pace momentarily to look back down the valley. In fact, it was the only moment of pure contentment I experienced on that mountain, and it's a feeling I tap into on those heavier days which we all have from time to time. And it fills me with pride. With joy. With unbridled emotion.

There were 100 porters in front of me and 35 Irish people behind me, and there I was, Enda 2.0, in the middle of it all, complete with the washing machine and it was magical. And I allowed myself the following thought: 'I did this. I made this happen.' It was a super feeling. It's still a super feeling.

During the trek, I had patches where I was 'on' and then 'off'. I journeyed from one end of the wellness spectrum to the other, but there was some consolation to be drawn from the fact that pretty much everyone was in the same boat. We climbed together, we ate together and a lot of us got sick together. As for the toilet breaks, think toil rather than toilet. We might have been climbing a volcano with a dormant cone – Kibo (5,895 metres) – one which hasn't erupted for approximately 360,000 years, but we were enduring some pretty violent eruptions of our own.

There were Irish-made biohazards all along the Shira Route: we had toilets marked with X's all along the trail given the extent of the diarrhoea and vomiting. A lot of them simply couldn't be used given the levels of violently evacuated infection risks they contained. It was crazy stuff at times; I really was left wondering where it was all coming from. Feeling like crap took on a whole new meaning on the highest free-standing mountain on the planet. This was an attack on the senses the likes of which none of us could draw a previous personal comparison with. And all the while, the air was growing thinner, the lungs were working harder, and every sense and nerve ending was under attack.

Trying to stay hygienic amidst the excreta and stomach lining also threw up a conundrum for me, something I hadn't anticipated prior to our departure from Londorossi Gate (3,050m) on day one. I didn't foresee my being an alcoholic among the myriad of matters I had to contend with in the jungle; it wasn't as if there was an 'offy' available for a detour. But having to wash my hands with alcohol-based disinfectant 20 times a day absolutely fried my brain. 'Hello darkness, my old friend.' The way my mind and body were working by then was akin to a violently backfiring car still in motion but coughing up plumes of fumes, and that hand sanitiser might as well have been a bottle of vodka. An unexpected serpent in Eden. Raw alcohol on my hands between 20 and 25 times a day, for a man who at that point hadn't had a drink for 11 years, was problematic to put it mildly, but I had to endure it. It was all that stood between me and further vomiting, vicious stomach cramps and all that comes with the latter.

The environment, spectacular and all as it was, was difficult to comprehend. On day one, we were opening our tents and looking down on the clouds. By the time we reached Barranco Camp, we were three days away from the clouds beneath us! As the trail grew steeper and our collective fatigue grew deeper, the jadedness pulsing through my leadened feet was like wet concrete slowly setting in a sock.

My mind was jumping between memory, reality and, to be honest, a touch of fear. I went from thoughts of socks and concrete to all the way back home. Waterford. Blaas. Large bottles (no thanks, you know the history). 'Well, boy.' The top of the town. Wit as arid as the Atacama dust. 'It was chaos, Billy'.[†] De La Salle College. The unbridled joy of opening the front door at home and leaving the day and outside world behind you as it shut. The early morning chat with Maeve. The joy of it. The generosity of so many people I'd befriended through my Belfast–Waterford walk and this latest escapade. The crowds on The Quay when we completed the walk. The struggle to comprehend what we'd done. The drive to take on something else. The will and purpose to do something to help people in the darkest, most soul-crushing of mindsets. Amidst all those images and sensations, I was 'beamed' back to our official starting point, surely the first time that the carpark at Tesco Ardkeen (in the city), a short washing machine walk from our house, had served as the first collective steps taken in a summit attempt of Mount Kilimanjaro. Maybe we should put a commemorative plaque there to mark the spot!

We had left Ardkeen at 11 a.m. on a Monday morning. The following evening at 6 p.m. we got to our hotel in Tanzania, and that trip was a marathon in its own right. The next morning, we were out the door of the hotel and straight out onto a mountain that would prove both befriender and bedraggler. The relationship between the mountain and I soon became a Liz Taylor–Richard Burton thing: we didn't know if we should cosy up together or contact our respective legal teams.

But every forward step still represented progress. We all knew what we had to do, we had some semblance of the enormity of the effort, but with Maeve out there with me too, and taking 33 other people's welfare into account, I had a lot going on. Everyone on the trek was there of their own volition, but they were all there because of my idea, and as

---

† A famous declaration by a caller on local radio station WLR, proffered to the late and sadly missed presenter, Billy McCarthy.

much as I felt proud when gazing back down the Karanga Valley, there was pressure too. Rightly or wrongly, I felt responsible for everybody and I had to spare some thought to how I would deal with a misfortune befalling anyone during the trek, including death. A paper produced by Marcus Hauser, titled 'Deaths Due to High-Altitude Illness among Tourists Climbing Mount Kilimanjaro', revealed that 25 people died on the mountain between 1996 and 2003. And while the authority which runs the Kilimanjaro Park is the only body with the official annual fatality figure, given that the numbers climbing the mountain are doubling each year, it's been recently estimated that the mountain takes between six and seven tourists annually. Hauser's study was tourist-specific – it didn't take porters, who outnumber tourists by three to one on most treks – into account, so the annual death rate is, in all likelihood, higher than seven: it could well be double that. One report I looked through once safely home estimated that half of all those trekking Kilimanjaro will develop some level of mountain sickness, with one in 50 climbers developing 'something serious'. Given how otherworldly the geography and the entire experience proved, 'something serious' had to be expected, but it was impossible to anticipate what that meant once reality, and volcanically violent illness, struck on the slopes.

Yet amidst the carcass-seeking vultures, the biohazard portaloos and red-dotted eyes, I saw the very best in humanity. I've followed sport throughout my life, but I never truly saw heroism until I hit that mountain. This was a group of people who were on the physical, emotional and mental precipice, with nothing left to give. But they kept going. And the more pressure they were under, the more they were squeezed, the more evident their character became. Their positivity shone through. They were 'Sharing the Load', and, like the carbon in diamonds, they grew brighter and brighter. And the summit drew ever nearer.

10

Summit Story – Part Two

'I drank and took drugs because I am a drug addict and an alcoholic. I'm not cured. You don't get cured. I haven't had a drink or a pill in six-and-a-half years, which isn't to say I won't have one tomorrow ... The problem is, I don't want a drink. I want ten drinks. Because I'm an alcoholic ... [and] it's very hard to understand.'

Leo McGarry, *The West Wing*[5]

The 'me and my washing machine' metaphor was literally all about walking from Point A to Point B. But the physical journey I'd committed to between Belfast and Waterford, mighty and all as it was, was just a component of the slightly mad escapades I've embarked on since my reboot.

It's been about what I've committed to away from the classroom, how I've maintained my climb out of the bottle, embracing sobriety while recalibrating my addictive sensibility, all of which has helped me to take my place upon the larger canvas we can all paint on if we keep our minds open to the ambition of fulfilling a dream. But the past few years have also represented an enormous mental and emotional journey for me, and the realisation that my mental health is something I have to work on regularly. I had to grapple with the notion that having a breakdown after my last drink, having accepted that I was an alcoholic, wasn't necessarily a once-off.

Most people, and this is just how I see it, don't realise that your mental health isn't a cast-iron continuum: you will have good days and bad days, no matter who you are and how strong you are. For me, I've learned coping skills along the way, be it in those initial weeks after my last drink, walking along the eastern Irish seaboard or leading a team of lionhearts up the unforgiving slopes of Kilimanjaro. I know my triggers and I know how to avoid them. And I do know if the wheels come off that I've got it within me to put them back on again. And that's a crucial difference between me now and me in the midst of binge drinking, enveloped by the alcohol-soaked delusion that I was okay, that I was indestructible. In that respect, the washing machine and all that's come with it has been as much a life-altering leveller as it's proven a life-changing enhancer. The friendships I've made on my Pieta Challenges are difficult to quantify there's been so many. I've got more genuine friendships now in my late 40s than I had in my early 20s. What I've learned about myself and what I've realised I'm capable of has proven just as illuminating and enriching, and I clung to those learnings as I wiped the pure alcohol between my fingers on the Shira Route, persuading myself with every step that I could withstand each sensation that this brutal, colon-weakening ascent was dragging me through. And all of those collected and shared experiences were willing me up the mountain.

My mind was like a mass of tangled electrical cable on the ascent – real Christopher Nolan 'flashback within a flashback' stuff – but the cables were connected where they needed to be at either end when it came to keeping everything operable, so I went with it as best I could. In the slow blink of a jaded eye, I was back at the base of the mountain, driving through the entrance to Machame Park (1,800m) where we saw 100 Tanzanian porters who climb up and down the mountain each and every week, with the sort of lung capacity anyone singing at La Scala would be envious off, and they catch sight of this pasty-faced Paddy clambering out of a bus with a washing machine. 'What the hell' was written all over their faces. And while we got our lunch and sorted out some paperwork, in the distance I could see all of the porters heading over to the washing machine, picking it up, trying it on and having a big snigger about it all – and that was lovely to see.

As the week went on, the porters' respect for what we were doing and why we were doing it grew all the more evident. It became clear to them that we weren't just climbing Kilimanjaro for the craic. We were climbing it to save lives in Ireland and the fact that the washing machine was heavier than what they were carrying, which must have been a whole new experience for them, brought it home to them that what we were doing wasn't a joke in any way, shape or form.

When we reached the Karanga Valley, Denise Doyle and Peter Shanahan - both from Waterford - were going through the mill due to diarrhoea and headaches. I'd completed my walk and rather than rest up and try to somewhat relax, I went back towards the edge of this cliff near the camp; I knew they were 45 minutes to an hour behind us, and I was roaring down the valley, shouting 'Come on, ye can do this!' And as I was walking towards the cliff edge there were four porters sitting nearby, playing checkers after a day's work, when one of them says to me 'Share the load.' He might as well have handed me a million-Euro cheque.

By then, they'd stopped calling me Enda and went with the Swahili name they'd bestowed upon me instead - '*Adu Machine, Nguvu kama Simba*' (The Washing Machine Man, Strong like a Lion) - and that was incredible. I've never met people with such an appreciation and love of life, full of song, dance and humour - they even wrote and sang a song about me and the washing machine, 'The Lion and the Washing Machine Man' - and the courtesy they offered me, in addition to their companionship, blew me away. In addition to the sinew-weakening, lung-sanding altitude, I'd not anticipated the love and kindness our porters demonstrated, and if you believe that a stranger is simply a friend you've yet to meet, we lived that maxim on Kilimanjaro. And it was wonderful.

Identifying a highlight of the trip is akin to asking Pelé what his favourite goal was or which Oscar nomination Meryl Streep values above all others. But getting to share this experience with Maeve, who has seen me at my best and worst in ways no one else can understand, was life-enhancing, and I'd like to think it was for her too. And that crystallising moment wasn't catching a particular glimpse from her above the cloud line or re-living some scene from *Out of Africa* (even in my own mind!) that has stayed with me above all others. Her words are the ones I hang on anyway, but at one stage during the climb when I made my way back over to her - now I'm covered in dirt which is worth pointing out - I gave her a kiss and she said to me: 'If our kids have one per cent of your spirit, I'd be happy.' Right then, even if I was at sea level and could lift two washing machines over my head, you could have knocked me over with a leaf. It raised every goosebump I've ever had in my life that little bit higher, and it took me three hours to come down from that. It was an extraordinary moment. I didn't want to die on the mountain, I didn't want anyone coming home with serious injury or discomfort, but had it all ended for me, there and then, having my wife share those words with me would have left me at peace. Every day I had lived up to that point and every moment I had shared with Maeve took on a little more meaning for me. Don't ever tell me that words have no power.

Maeve, the smallest person in our group, was the first to reach the summit. You couldn't make it up. She, and everyone else who had reached the summit, had travelled two days just to get to Tanzania. They had walked uphill for six days and averaged seven to eight hours of hiking on each of those days. The smallest person in our group, who set off in the dark of an African night, made it to the top before anyone else did. What an extraordinary woman. She's made of titanium and proof, as if any were needed, that nobody should be judged by their physical stature. You can never reckon upon the level of resolve that lies inside anyone. And when push came to shove, on she went. My Maeve. And she made it to the top.

On summit day, you hike for four to five hours to get to Barrafu Camp. Once we got there, we had our lunch and then lay down to try to get some rest. The final stretch lay ahead. At 11 p.m. that night, having already put in a hard hike that day, we were off again, en route for the summit. Maeve and the group got back to the camp at 12.30 p.m. the next day: 19 hours of hiking in the space of a day, most of it at minus 15 degrees Celsius, in the dark, with less than 40 per cent oxygen. What they did was superhuman. Me? Well, the spirit was always willing, but the flesh proved too weak. I didn't reach the summit, and it still hurts like hell.

Brian Bateson and John Healy of the Earth's Edge adventure holiday group were our guides on the trek, and it fell to Brian to tell me that my race was run. He laid it on the line to me, and while I knew I was struggling, with systems breaking down from temple to toe-tip, I was desperate to get to the summit. Enda 2.0 doesn't do failures, and anything other than reaching the summit seemed impossible when we gathered in the car park at Ardkeen.

The lads' professionalism was difficult to appreciate amidst the light-headedness and vomiting, but the duty of care they showed to each and every one of us during every minute of this challenge was above and beyond. Typically, either of them would greet you in the morning and ask how you'd slept. And this wasn't for the sake of small talk. If you told them you'd had an iffy night, they'd be honed in on you all day on the mountain. They could tell when altitude was getting more problematic for any of us.

And every single night, Brian and John sat at the top of the table in both meal tents and it was only when I got home that I fully grasped what they were doing the entire time. If you didn't eat, they could tell your body was succumbing, surrendering even, to altitude. Ditto on the fluid front. And over the first two days, every one of us got a tongue-lashing for touching food without washing our hands. 'Diarrhoea will end your climb' became a mantra of theirs during those opening days. Offering each other sweets from a bag became a no-no, because if I put my hand into any of the lads' sweet bags, I was transferring bacteria – akin to the capuchin monkey in *Outbreak*. They were like primary school teachers, but in the best manner possible, as were the Tanzanian guides. '*Poli, poli*' is Swahili for taking something slowly, and if we tried to do anything at speed, even standing up, you had to take the '*poli, poli*' approach, and stand in three steps and really concentrate on your breathing. We were no longer bounding up the Comeraghs for training. Everything those guides did they did in our best interests. We weren't in Coumshingaun anymore, never mind Kansas.

Brian was such a calm presence when he broke the news to me, and he did it with such delicacy and kindness. He had to know how crestfallen I'd be when he laid out the facts. It was 5 a.m. I was as cold, tired and miserable as I'd ever felt in my life. But this wasn't alcohol-related breakdown misery. This was me at the closest I've ever been to total physical disassembly. The game was up and Brian had to break it to me. 'Enda, given your size, you're probably looking at a six- or seven-hour stretcher-carry down the mountain with four men carrying you.' Now he didn't say, 'don't do it' but he gave me the facts and I was lucid enough to know I was putting other people at risk if I continued.

The previous day, Brian had a private conversation with me and asked me how I was feeling. My immediate reply was 'yeah, I'm great', when he could obviously see I wasn't. In mountaineering terms, Brian was still playing poker whereas I could barely manage snap by then. Yet still I told him: 'I am desperate to get to the summit. I need to get that photo of me with the washing machine.'

Brian, who was the epitome of calm, replied:

'Enda, we need to keep you alive. If we keep you alive, the message that you're spreading is so powerful. It's got the potential to save other people's lives and to raise money for charity. It's important that we bring you back intact.'

And so I stopped. The end had come but thanks to medical best practice, I wasn't about to face the ultimate in final curtains. And so I recorded a two-minute video to capture the moment, well, for myself more than anyone else there, but also because the chances are I'd have forgotten exactly what I was thinking at that moment if I hadn't clicked 'record'. I knew a lot of people back home were following what we doing on Facebook, and while the clip looks to me in hindsight like an emotional middle-aged Paddy with the flu in a *Bohemian Rhapsody* outtake, this is what I said and felt when I knew my African adventure was over:

'So this is the video. The video I hoped I wouldn't have to make (spits, then sighs). Seven hours in, and, I don't know, two [hours] from the top. The doctor has said that my saturation level is too dangerous to continue and if I keep going, it will kill me. I'm gutted but it wasn't a slogan, "Share the Load". The strong guys who were with me, they've got my back. That washing machine is on its way to the surface [sic – I meant the summit of course]. That tricolour is with it, with my lovely wife and the brilliant people who raised all that money for Pieta will get that photo taken. It's ironic the way this has ended because if I don't share the load right now, it would cost me my life. (Blow out cheeks). I've three fantastic kids, a brilliant wife and family. Life is precious, so as much as it hurts me, I'll go back to camp, it's still five hours downhill, but it's downhill and I'll live to fight another day. If you're in trouble, ring 1800-247-247. Don't, eh, don't try climbing mountains with washing machines. Talk to you soon.'

Brian was effectively my conscience operating remotely when he put the four men, stretcher and potential death scenario to me. And how right he was. After all, what good would I have been to anyone had I popped my clogs on the top of the mountain? A man dying on a trek for a charity whose very reason for being is to preserve and champion life wouldn't have been the greatest PR move for Pieta House either, let's face it. We really couldn't have been in better hands. But Maeve was going on without me, and that provided a greater level of anxiety for me there and then than four men, a stretcher and the death notice on local radio.

I met Maeve on a Monday in October 1986. Two days later, I asked her to marry me. I knew. I just knew. Talk about Thunderbolt City, to go all *Four Weddings* about our romance. She's a physically stunning woman but, more importantly, she's an incredible person. She's 49, has a 22-year-old son and she's got a six-pack. She's incredibly healthy but she's such a kind soul and we're such good friends. We're married just shy of 25 years and she's everything to me. She's my soulmate. To know her truly is to love her, and if you've not got 'I feel it in my fingers, I feel it in my toes' running through your head right now, I may well have lost you. Forgive me the indulgence but my God, she's worth it.

Prior to the trip, we'd touched on some of the negative outcomes that could befall either of us on the mountain: we'd spoken about broken legs, one of us having to turn around on day one, two or three, and, yeah, we'd sat in bed and discussed death. What if one of us died on Kilimanjaro? And that was pretty good planning; I felt somewhat pre-armed before we hit the trail. But living and breathing the reality of oxygen saturation and my becoming a potential health risk was a different bag of jellies altogether. But when we had to say goodbye, both of us exhausted, as she pressed on for the summit and I headed down the mountain, the fear, the demons, visited me with a vengeance.

My default setting as Maeve's husband is always to be there for her and to catch her if she falls. That's all I've known since I was 19 years old. But seven to eight hours after we'd said our 'see you soons', over a crackly walkie-talkie, John Healy managed to get a message from the summit that Maeve was on her way back. She had summited! She'd stood on top of Africa! I knew she was safe and it was absolute magic. Maeve came down with one of the Tanzanian porters, along with Denise Doyle. The next day I gave that porter a couple of hundred dollars, which you're not supposed to do. It was probably a couple of months' wages for him, but he literally had wrapped her in cotton wool and taken her all the way back down to safety.

Maeve was the first to summit, perhaps out of the kindness of the rest of the group on approach to the top, but she was filmed, walking on and reaching the top, and I'll treasure that footage until the kids empty my urn on Tramore's Backstrand. It's her Neil Armstrong moment. She was down to about 10 steps a minute by then and you can see how physically devastated she was. And everyone who summited, even taking altitude sickness out of the equation, was struggling. One of the Tanzanian porters hauled the washing machine to the summit: talk about one giant leap for white goods! And I saw that image and it brought the tricolour I'd had in my sports bag during my months of training back into sharp focus. I'd dreamt about taking out the flag on the summit, and posing for a snap alongside the machine. I might have even broken into 'Amhrán na bFhiann' up there if the lungs had been up to it, but I didn't get that Kodak moment.

Rejection has led me to redirection. We raised over €150,000. I'd wanted to bring that washing machine to the summit myself but another

Irishman and a Tanzanian finished the job. My body had forced me to 'share the load' and I'd gotten into difficulties from as early as day two, so to get as far as I did, with sickness coming and going, wasn't that shabby an effort in hindsight. And when I removed my bruised ego from the equation, and thought about looking over my shoulder in the Karanga Valley, seeing everyone who had joined me on this escapade, and then watching them coming down a steep, sharp, rocky trail and into camp, layered in dirt, caked in dust and sweat, that extracted me from my own personal disappointment. Almost everybody was bleeding from their ears and via their noses, yet nobody carped or cribbed. There was stuff seeping out of orifices that even Ridley Scott hadn't packed into *Alien*, scabby balls of congealed mucus which had erupted from shredded respiratory systems following cough after cough after cough. It was crazy but it was quite wonderful.

Catching a glimpse of Maeve on her return to the camp was like seeing her on that Monday in October 1986. Thunderbolt City revisited. I walked up towards her; Martin Molloy was nearby so I asked him to make a video of the moment. I'd had some coffee and some food by then so I was coming around, and I was quite emotional. I don't think the emotion was quite reciprocated simply because Maeve had nothing left. Anyone who sat down when they got back didn't move for at least an hour. Some of the group were carried back to camp, and needed help having their underwear removed just to go to the bathroom. People were at their physical limit, but nobody was in grave danger, which spoke volumes for the care and oversight our guides offered.

The merit of any physical test is the challenge it poses. You strive to meet that challenge when you're training, let alone when you're in the thick of a trek. And if it doesn't challenge you, then it doesn't change you. We could have helicoptered someone over the summit, winched them out, stuck on an oxygen tank and enjoyed the African sunrise. But where's the challenge in that? Dragging your ass up a mountain having trained and fundraised for a year: now that was a challenge. I'm no fan of suffering, but if you look at anything you take on in life, be it painting a bedroom, organising a wedding, climbing Kilimanjaro or any life event that involves stress and effort, the prospect of things going wrong, overcoming adversity, that's where the joy is. That's where the victory is.

We returned home like war veterans, brothers and sisters bound by a shared experience. Until you've slept on a 40-degree slope on rocky ground for nine days, and until you've woken up in the middle of the night and seen an 'X' marked on a toilet contaminated with diarrhoea, it's very hard to describe it to other people. This experience has become such a huge part of our lives and it always will be. Yet it's hard to express the reality of what it actually was to prepare for it, to take it on, and to collectively come home safely, having raised a huge amount of money. And I hope these words have conveyed, even in part, what it was like to take on Africa's highest mountain with a washing machine.

As for how I can top an experience like this? Easily, believe it or not, but with urgency and great planning. The grass won't grow under these feet again. These challenges are my antidepressants. I want to do them. I need to do them. Another adventure is a necessity, as it's part of my regime.

> 'This guy's walking down a street when he falls in a hole. The walls are so steep, he can't get out. A doctor passes by, and the guy shouts up, "Hey you, can you help me out?" The doctor writes a prescription, throws it down in the hole and moves on. Then a priest comes along, and the guy shouts up, "Father, I'm down in this hole, can you help me out?" The priest writes out a prayer, throws it down in the hole and moves on. Then a friend walks by. "Hey Joe, it's me, can you help me out?" And the friend jumps in the hole. Our guy says, "Are you stupid? Now we're both down here." The friend says, "Yeah, but I've been down here before, and I know the way out."'

These words, again from *The West Wing*'s Leo McGarry, spoke to me in a manner similar, I suspect, to the late actor John Spencer, who played the role. He knew the reality of alcoholism, of recovery, and of the compulsive search for fulfilment, to fill time with something other than alcohol. That's my life too. Life as a sober man has provided me with a whole different range of challenges. But I've embraced them all. And that's why there'll be further adventures – but not at altitude mind you! I've chosen life. And it's magical.

11

Sweeping the Room

It's a Saturday night in a *Downton Abbey*-type London hotel. I'm about to address Tripadvisor's world sales team and I am absolutely buzzing. I find myself standing in front of a group of the very best in their respective fields, and life feels pretty damn good. I get into my speechifying mode, the crowd giggle at my gags, they're invested in my story (well, I didn't spot too many eyes gravitating towards their phones while I spoke) and they appear to enjoy both my company and the strength of my message.

My speech ends, the 'Trip Advisees' applaud and head for the bar while I shut down my computer. As one set of professionals leave the room, another less heralded group of professionals enter; the hotel floor staff, mostly Eastern European, move in to clear away the dishes and glasses, so I join them. It's nothing dramatic or too philanthropic on my behalf, but I pick up maybe a half-dozen glasses and a couple of plates. And as I was doing that, one of Tripadvisor's top brass re-enters the function room, sees what I'm doing and asks why. 'I'm sweeping the room,' I replied, a phrase he wasn't familiar with at all.

It's a concept which the New Zealand rugby team embraced during Richie McCaw's record-breaking captaincy. You might well be at the top of your sport, or, as I'd been for 90 minutes that evening in London, the focal point in that function room, but when I finished what I was there to do, I wanted to do even a light level of 'sweeping'. It's a means of keeping one's self grounded, even during those times in life when it feels like the good times are in perpetual motion. One of the floor staff was similarly perplexed by what I was doing and said to me: 'That's our job; our manager will kill us if he sees you doing what we should be doing.'

To which I replied:

> 'Oh, it's not about you at all and please don't take any offence. This is about me, it's something I do when I speak in places like this. I like to put away a few chairs or stack up some plates. It's a reflex, more than anything.'

The look of surprise on the staff's faces, in addition to that of the Trip Advisee who came back into the room to see their suited and booted VIP guest for the evening helping to stack away glasses, is a pleasant memory. It makes me feel good about myself and reminds me about the importance of enjoying big nights like that, working a room and winning over an audience, but to never get too carried away by it. That small distance between a pat on the back and a kick in the arse is something I've never lost sight of. The need to retain humility and perspective remains a constant in my life. I could have been foolhardy and, against sounder medical judgement, made it to the summit of Kilimanjaro. I could well have dragged my weakened body up there; the obsessive in me that propelled me into liquor for so long might just have eked those final few hours of grunt out of me. Granted, had I done so, the odds on me being brought back home in a casket would have been significantly increased. A literal dead cert, if you will.

But the washing machine reaching the summit was what the trip was about; it wasn't about me ferrying it all the way up there. That was a cheque even I couldn't guarantee my ego could cash. I literally embodied 'Sharing the Load' on the side of that mountain. I may not have succeeded personally, but the message won out. And I'm totally fine with that.

A lot of people set out to achieve goals in life, but a great many of them stop pursuing that goal, give up on that goal or get so disillusioned with life that the goal itself evaporates from both view and recollection. If you've lost track of your goal, I suspect it's because your 'why', your reason for establishing it as a goal in the first place, wasn't strong enough. I've always been driven by the why. The why is so important to me. It gives me huge energy and motivation for everything else in life, in addition to achieving the goal itself. The insight of former Donegal senior football manager Jim McGuinness springs to mind when he wrote about why his All-Ireland winning panel might be training at 80 per cent of their ability when the goal is to play with the full ton. Flat out. All or nothing.

'Then we would go again and we would keep stopping and starting until we all knew that they were moving at the absolute maximum their bodies would permit. Part of it was to improve fitness but, more important, it was about getting them to see that they could shake off their inhibitions and just go for it. People are afraid. People are afraid to just leave it out there in case they are judged negatively. It is human nature. We hold back even though the most exhilarating and liberating thing you can do in your life is to just put yourself out there. So in DCU and in Ballybofey and on the beach in Dunfanaghy, that was the question the boys began to address for themselves: What is holding you back? People aren't often asked that question in life and it is a simple one. It is at the heart of so much.'[6]

'What is holding you back?' I pencilled around that question while reading McGuinness' award-winning memoir; desecrating books with my own etchings has been one of my 'MOs', so lending me a book isn't advisable unless a slightly revised design upon its return comes as a request. Obsessiveness goes hand in hand with addictive behaviour. And part of my Enda 2.0 obsessiveness manifests itself in my planning levels. Jesus, do I love a good plan. Verbally, I'd tell you when the event is on, what time it's on at and I tend to talk out my ideas a lot. Planning, followed by some re-planning, has been one of the elements which has helped make Belfast to Waterford and Kilimanjaro such tremendous successes.

A lot of people tend to wait until something significant goes wrong in their lives before conducting a review or post-mortem. But just consider the difference even a small mindshift would make or doing what I've come to embrace in my sobriety: the pre-mortem, e.g. having a call put into a hotel about their having a second projector in the event that their main model doesn't work during one of my presentations. By reducing the variables, you create a greater environment of certainty. It's why a soccer team practicing penalties in the event of a shoot-out is essentially pre-empting a potential game-time scenario. It may not guarantee your team victory when all of the variables of such a scenario are accounted for: players still on the pitch, fatigue levels, stadium atmosphere, which end the spot kicks will be taken at, etc. But you've increased your odds of succeeding: by preparing.

I'm a huge fan of the Nike slogan, 'Just Do It'. It's such a simple message but, in a way, it answers Jim McGuinness' question. To execute, to act on something, to drive a change by being the change yourself is, to quote Rocky Balboa, 'how winning is done'. And just as there's no such thing as a stupid question, seeking advice from those with a greater knowledge base across the range of varied disciplines I've dipped my toes into is one of the many ways in which I try to improve myself, be it physical training or communication skills. While 'Share the Load' has become one of my mental health mantras, finding people you can counterbalance your life with, be it professionally or personally, involves positive communication. And I think one of the reasons I've had such a great marriage with Maeve is how we complement each other's weaknesses and we look after each other through our strengths.

I'll give you a practical example: I don't know how much of the mortgage is paid, or how much is left on it. I've been teaching for 25 years and I don't know what I earn each month. I don't know my bank account number. I am, always have been, and forever shall be useless in such matters. That's Maeve's area, and that dominion shall forever be hers.

However, I possess a whole set of skills where I feel I'm overflowing with moxie, and that's something which Maeve has always recognised in me – thankfully! For my part, I've always recognised what I've needed to succeed by cooperating and tapping into the knowhow of other like-minded people, albeit with differing skillsets, and that's why team efforts such as the two big walks have worked so well.

As Dr Bob Rotella put it:

> 'The lesson for people striving to be exceptional is not to try to do it completely alone. You're going to need other people on board with you. You need to select those people carefully, and you need to treat them right... Those people must believe in you and your talent.'[7]

The togetherness, the sense of a shared experience and the collegiality which emerges through mutual suffering is a most beautiful thing – but let's hope there's no mass bowel evacuating come our next grand adventure.

Surveying your life and identifying the capacity that exists within yourself to bring about positive and sustainable change is something Bob Rotella also touched on in his bestselling book, *How Champions Think*:

'Exceptional people in my experience are almost always very good at monitoring and evaluating their adherence to a good process and catching themselves when they slip slightly – when they're just half an inch away from where they should be. Average people let themselves get a lot further off track before they catch themselves… The exceptional person monitors himself in relation to these goals (though not, of course, in the heat of competition) and uses that evaluation for making course corrections. The question of how good someone can be is only answered after the individual has put in a long period of sustained, committed adherence to a process of improvement. By "a long period", I don't mean days or weeks or even months. Typically, a long period might mean years.'[8]

There are phases in all of our lives when we feel we don't have what we need. Now you can choose to sit there and wear a permanent shawl of resigned misery or you can make a positive choice. This is a point I've regularly shared with the kids I teach, as well as those I work with: you can choose to focus on the problem or you can choose to focus on creating a solution for those problems. Get up a half-hour earlier every morning. Stack some chairs. Sweep the room. Improvisation is a real-life skill that people need to have. When someone says to me that they haven't got the time to exercise or to study, I reply by asking what have they done to make the time, to carve out that space in which they can progress, grow and achieve.

If you tell me that you can't afford something, my follow-up is two-pronged: what are you doing to generate additional income and what are you putting away each week or month to help you to get where you need to be financially?

Improvising can play a part in reaching your ideal destination. Seeking expert advice can help too. It's a darn sight better than shrugging your shoulders and accepting the status quo as your lot in life.

Achieving something entirely independently is a rare feat: after all, Hannibal couldn't have traversed the Alps without those elephants, or his army for that matter. Teamwork makes accomplishing a dream so much easier, and that was one of my over-arching afterthoughts in the months following the Kilimanjaro trek.

John Wooden defined team spirit as:

'[being willing to lose] oneself in the group for the good of the group. It means being not just willing but eager to sacrifice

> personal interest or glory for the welfare of all. There is a profound difference between mere willingness and eagerness. A prisoner on a chain gang may be willing to break rocks to avoid punishment. But how eager is he? Of course, we all want to do well and receive individual praise. Yes, that's fine, if you put it to use for the good of the team, whatever your team is: sports, business, family, or community. Team spirit means you are willing to sacrifice personal considerations for the welfare of all. That defines a team player.'9

For me, the most profound success of Kilimanjaro has been the spark of other people's energies, a whole host of individual human elements which blended so well on the side of a mountain half the world away from Waterford. The differences within a group can ultimately provide enduring strength, and that same dynamic equally applies within a marriage. Maeve is everything I'm not and to me, when I reflect on us as a team, I feel that's why we work. I'm loud, brash, in your face and love attention: she's quiet, shy and is very happy to be in the background. But what we have works, and it's wonderful.

Success in team sports is rarely achieved without the presence of an enforcer, an assassin (sometimes a combination of the aforementioned), a magician and a grafter. Show me Lionel Messi and I'll show you Carles Puyol. Show me Ronan O'Gara and I'll show you John Hayes. Show me Henry Shefflin and I'll show you Noel Hickey. For that matter, show me Ernest Shackleton and I'll show you Tom Crean. Throughout my active alcoholism – I remain an addict and I'll never lose sight of that – Maeve remained at my side, my anchor during many squalls and hurricanes. And to see her as part of a bigger team, be it on the road between Belfast and Waterford, or enduring the wear and tear of an African mountain trek, underlined, to me, my good fortune to be her husband. I'll never have a more valuable teammate in life. Better together? Yes, yes, and yes again.

***

Now here's a question: if you could do anything in the world and not fail, what would you do – and I rarely meet someone who hasn't an answer to that – because we can all dream. But the problem is that we match those dreams, and indeed override them, with negative thoughts and actions: for example, I'd love to be a movie star but I've never been in a play. The biggest factor in not making things happen is in not taking action. Second to that, for me, is a lack of persistence. Many people ask me about what they should do if something goes wrong, but, for me, the going wrong is where success can and will ultimately arise from. You go again and then you go again until you've broken the tape, swam an ocean, carried a washing machine for a ludicrous distance, etc. I don't have an off switch nowadays. I've learned to face down rejection: I'll go with redirection instead. If you convince yourself of 'sin é' (that's it) and believe what's in front of you represents an insurmountable obstacle and that's me done for, then you've got a self-fulfilling prophecy on your hands. Dreaming outrageously might well lead to outrageous failure, but surely it's better to think about scaling that wall to see what's on the other side as opposed to white-flagging it all and withdrawing?

Someone who always dreamt big is John O'Shea, one of De La Salle College's most famous alumni. He is as solid as they come, with 119 international caps, five Premier League titles, a Champions League medal and a distinguished career he can draw just pride from, and that solidity was just as evident in the late 90s before a move to Manchester United beckoned. Back then, the dream of making the grade in England took level pegging to his Leaving Certificate studies, but if you asked him 20 years ago what his goals were it wasn't simply to play professional football, but to play at the highest level, at a club like Manchester United, in addition to an international career with Ireland. Now he was never brash in stating such an intention: John was steadfast and serious in his pursuit of achieving those dreams. There's never been a sensationalist bone in his body, as his career has subsequently testified. John was the ultimate professional before he ever signed forms with United, such was the confidence, charisma and strength he exuded as a teenager.

And to anyone who had noted John's progress back then with Waterford Bohemians, the success he has subsequently achieved was never really in doubt. John was a winner joining a winning machine, spearheaded by an extraordinary manager who had seen Sir Matt Busby's feats, bettered them and earned a knighthood of his own. John O'Shea exudes decency and honesty, something his parents, Jim (RIP) and Mary, ought to be particularly proud of. He dreamt big, he diligently pursued his dreams and in so doing became one of the most decorated players in the history of Irish soccer. And that John ended his international career donning the captain's armband will have surprised none of those who coached him at De La Salle. And it would be a considerable surprise if a decorated career in coaching doesn't lie ahead of him.

A sustained commitment to learning will undoubtedly drive John O'Shea onward now his playing days are over. The willingness to absorb fresh information, the willingness to face down physical and mental stagnation, committing one's self to not only acknowledge change but embrace it, is key to sustained growth.

My first ten minutes in the gym every morning, as I'm loosening out the limbs on a rowing machine, is a time I've come to devote to learning; 'Eye of the Tiger' isn't oscillating my semi-circular canals, I can assure you. I use that warm-up time to listen to a podcast, a book review or a meditation. So if I'm in the gym six times a week, then I've enjoyed an hour of learning, working the brain first before working the body to the point that I'm dripping streams of sweat, and the combination of both has provided a path to inner revelation. It's opened my mind to the concept that I can and will continue to improve, as a teacher, as an athlete, as a guest speaker, as a parent and as a husband: fuel for the soul in a way that brandy and milk could never, ever be.

Roman Emperor Marcus Aurelius, during one of his many *Meditations*, professed:

> 'While it's true that someone can impede our actions, they can't impede our intentions and our attitudes, which have the power of being conditional and adaptable. For the mind adapts and converts any obstacle to its action into a means of achieving it. That which is the impediment to action is turned to advanced action. The obstacle on the path becomes the way.'

My addictive personality has steered me down two paths: one that was utterly self-destructive while the other has steered my life into a series of madcap, magical endeavours and the company of a whole new range of friends and acquaintances. My life, as is, is one I could never have countenanced while skulling far too many shorts far too regularly. And that internal reflex of mine, the switch that goes off at the end of a speech and propels me onto the function room floor to stack away a few seats, is the reality check which keeps me humble. It also serves as a happy reminder that no matter how far I've come and no matter where I've carried that washing machine, that I'm no better than anyone else. I'm just the best version of myself. And that's enough for me. When I think about the slow-motion suicide attempt that my drinking days, in hindsight, have come to represent, it's more than enough.

**

'Drink to me, drink to my health, you know I can't drink anymore...'
                                                    Pablo Picasso's last words

C-3PO: 'Sir, the possibility of successfully navigating an asteroid field is approximately three thousand, seven hundred twenty to one!'
Han Solo: 'Never tell me the odds!'

The Empire Strikes Back

Peter Freuchen is my kind of guy. He packed a lot in over the course of his life and while he didn't quite make the 28,000-day mark which constitutes the average human life nowadays (he died in 1957, aged 71), he lived a life that makes carrying a washing machine towards the summit of Kilimanjaro feel like a 'Couch to 5K' challenge.

Possessing an Indiana Jones-type spirit in a Chewbacca-sized body (he stood all of 6'7", weighing over 300lbs and was married three times), the Danish-born explorer truly wrung each drop out of life. And the more I discovered about Freuchen, the more I came to admire this bear of a man and his astounding spirit.

During an expedition in Iceland in 1926, Freuchen was effectively entombed by an avalanche, and it hit him so hard that he rolled into a ball, only for the snow and ice to compact right around him. By the time the avalanche stopped, he attempted to dig himself out only to discover that the ice was so compacted that his fingernails were chiselled off in the process. He was encased in what amounted to a concrete orb. Even Rasputin might have waved the white flag given the dilemma Freuchen found himself in. So he sat there for three hours; he could feel the hypothermia kicking in and he knew he was dying. And what happened next is not only disgusting but it revealed this man's ability to look beyond failure, to see that there is a superhuman quality which I feel sits deep inside all of us, but few of us are prepared to realise, whatever the odds.

Three hours into his living nightmare, Peter Freuchen, encased in snow and ice, opened his trousers and defecated into his own hand. And with his own waste, he formed it into a chisel - something he'd seen those native to the Arctic do with the frozen poop of their sled dogs - so he created a shank from his own excrement, sharpened it, waited for it to freeze and then dug himself out with a tool hewn from his own stool. And, amazing as that is in itself, the story didn't end there.

Freuchen couldn't stand up - his toes were frostbitten - and he crawled for several hours until he reached the basecamp, by which time everyone else involved in the expedition had left - they assumed he had literally perished in the avalanche. But when Freuchen reached the camp, he examined his toes, by which time were completely black and permanently deprived of blood flow. He knew the next stage was gangrene, followed by death. So he took out a pair of pliers and removed his toes. Another account of his survival says he then ate what he amputated, and this explains why there's an oil portrait of Freuchen hanging above a fireplace in the trophy room of the New York Explorers Club, with a 'peg leg' clearly on display.

This remarkable man went on to write over 30 books, including *The Book of the Eskimos*, which was published posthumously in 1961, in which Freuchen detailed what it took to survive that avalanche. In 1933, he starred in and co-wrote an MGM movie, titled *Eskimo*, based on two of his own previously published books - it would win the following year's (inaugural) Academy Award for editing. He learned the Inuit culture during the course of his adventures and in 1911 he married a native woman, Navarana Mequpaluk - a relationship which was frowned upon south of the Arctic Circle at the time. They had a boy and a girl before Navarana died in 1921 during the Spanish Flu epidemic; he fell out with the Church as they wouldn't permit her burial in a Christian graveyard, as she was not baptised, so Peter went ahead and buried his wife himself.

A Jew, and a man who knew a bully when he saw one, Freuchen was involved in the Danish resistance to Nazi Germany during World War II and avoided execution by escaping to Sweden and, in turn, the United States. A year before the Axis was finally defeated, his 20-year marriage to margarine heiress Magdalene Vang Lauridsen had ended and by 1945 he'd made the acquaintance of and married a fashion illustrator named Dagmar Cohn, with whom he was famously photographed by Irving Penn. In the picture, Cohn sits diminutively to the left of the towering Freuchen, who is magnificently sporting a bearskin: and yes, he killed the bear and made a coat out of the trophy he proudly posed in.

And just when you'd be forgiven for thinking this guy's life had run out of wacky hairpin bends, in 1956, he appeared on the US TV gameshow *The $64,000 Question* and won it! A few months later, Freuchen received a Gold Medal from the International Benjamin Franklin Society for his 'service to mankind in opening new frontiers' before he died in 1957 following a heart attack. What a life, and what a headache the pattern of Freuchen's life must have posed for the writer charged with penning his obituary.

People like Peter Freuchen inspire me, and remind me why following a dream is worth pursuing. We should all dream the impossible dream and strive to run where the brave dare not go. We should give ourselves permission to chase and achieve the maddest and most inconceivable of goals.

But in this frenzied, overly busy world we live in, it appears a lot of us, whether we're students or adults, have lost the ability or discarded the willingness to dream the impossible dream.

If I gave you a choice between achieving a goal or fulfilling a dream, I'm willing to wage one Danish metahuman's amputated leg that the realisation of a dream is what you would opt for. Why have Butlins when you can have Disneyland instead? Technically, of course, one can argue that both represent the one and same outcome but there's something about that word, 'dream' - it catapults me into faster, higher, stronger territory. And I regularly say to teams, businesses and individuals that we should allow ourselves to dream the maddest of things.

When I'm sitting with a student for a study skills lesson, for example, the first question I'll put to them is about what job they'd most like, leaving exams out of the equation. Generally, I'm greeted by a reaction which suggests that they cannot compute what they're being asked. It's as if people have lost the ability to dream about ascending the summit, reaching for the stars, of remembering what they wanted above all else, however fanciful that might have been, before they even made double figures. There's a sense of imprisonment in students when I hear them talk about the CAO, the HDip, the Masters, the Doctorate: they're readily identifying the obstacles standing between them and their dream rather than seeing them as stepping stones to fulfilment. So what I tend to do when I encounter that sort of personality is to remove such obstacles and just ask the same question that this same person would have readily answered aged eight or nine: what do you want to be? I had one student tell me he'd love to be an architect, but before he draws his next breath he's telling me he'll never get the points he needs to pursue it at third level. But we should dream. We ought to keep dreaming. Give yourself permission to have the maddest and most ambitious of thoughts.

When I'm working with teams or businesses, another question I ask them to reflect on is: why not us? Why not me? Why should I not be the one who gets to that particular destination? A lot of us are very good at sitting on the couch, remote from the action and commenting on how good some footballer on the plasma screen is, or comment upon how good a certain writer or journalist is. But how did they get there? They must have had some doubt or disappointment along the way, but they still got where they wanted to more than anything in life. And something I've picked up on when working with sports stars or celebrities is just how ordinary they are. They're just ordinary people. We're all just ordinary people. But not all of us have dreams and it's something we should allow ourselves permission to cherish instead of being so harsh on ourselves.

Human nature being what it is, and having been culturally blitzkrieged for centuries about our imperfections and frailties - all at the expense of extolling the strengths and qualities which we all possess but often struggle to identify - it's no surprise that some of us don't tread softly enough. It's no surprise that cynicism is so pervasive. It's no surprise that fear of the bogeyman has influenced so many recent elections. It's no surprise that we decommission dreaming and disengage from positive 'whatiffery'. It's no surprise that most of us can rattle off our weaknesses without drawing breath, but will struggle when asked to list our strengths.

But if you're consistently failing at your goals, it's probably because, deep down, in your heart of hearts, you'll surely conclude it didn't matter enough to you. Sometimes we pick a goal which we feel other people think we ought to have, or we choose the more socially acceptable model, which means we're counteracting our own intent. We're not being honest with ourselves. We're not delving into the deepest reaches of our heart and soul until we reach down, deep within ourselves and unearth that world-class dream from which motivation flows to the point where our dream is not beyond our reach. Bill Shakespeare was on the money: 'To thine own self be true.'

Now a lot of this might sound a bit too sunny, even Californian for some people's tastes, but context helps too. Reality can be such a grind that it's good to dream, to allow yourself to enter a ringfenced space where life's serrated edges remain alien. Sitting in hospital with Maeve's mother, Anne, who has Alzheimer's, offers a perfect reminder to me that it's good to dream. It's good to have a comfort blanket we can throw over ourselves when we need it. It reminds me that when people ask me how I am, I consciously avoid that most particular of Irish replies, 'ah sure, I'm not too bad'. Anne's body is still there, but the essence of what made her a person, what made her an individual, is gone. She has no opportunity to dream, to think about what could lie ahead, to consider how she could succeed or even to consider failure. She can't do any of that anymore. She's a shell of a person, and it's heart-breaking to see. After one of those hospital visits, Maeve and I both said, almost in duet, that we're going to take an extra holiday or that we'll take another mind-boggling adventure in the next couple of years, as an attempt to fill the void in our family's lives.

And that brings me back to those 28,000 days most of us are fortunate to be granted. When I'm sat in an exam hall, or addressing a seminar in which I'll bullet-point, PowerPoint and wisecrack my way through for a few hours, it's possible to forget that the clock is ticking the whole time. Life should still happen, even when you're busy making plans.

Before the African trip, I was sitting with a journalist and I was mentioning how busy I was at the time, and in reply he said something along the lines of this:

'Jesus, Enda, you live your life as if you're terminally ill.'

And I immediately replied: 'I am.'

Now this really put the frighteners on the guy; I could see the colour draining from his face within seconds. 'Christ, the editor never told me this; oh, well, erm, ooh, I don't have to ask you about anything to do with that. That's probably a matter you'd prefer to keep private for both you and your family's sakes.'

But I told him: 'But you are too. Sure we're all going to die. You, me, the whole shooting gallery.'

It doesn't matter how much quinoa you eat; it doesn't matter how many times you run up and down the hill next to your house in circulation-limiting Lycra; the cloaked man with the scythe will tap on your door sometime down the line. You're going to the graveyard ultimately or, in my case, the beach in Tramore, on the bend towards the Back Strand, with the Saleens just a slip of water away. Don't tell me that's not a better place for your family to come and remember you than a field full of 'here lieth' slabs of marble. *Cremation and the Beach* might sound like an indie band's difficult second album, but that's my endgame once time cries halt to this crazy gallop.

And we should not only have dreams, but we should pursue our dreams because of that mightiest of constraints. Time is finite. And for far too many people, that cognisance comes too late to do something about our dreams. And the great irony, for me, is that taking on big adventures and wild challenges postpones not only our physical endgame, but the death of your soul, the death of your spirit; the death of the element that makes you different to the person on your left and the person on your right.

I once heard a man on radio talking about loneliness, something which has become a more prevalent feature in Irish life at a time when our population is increasing at its fastest rate since the pre-Famine era. He spoke about the importance of having dreams, the need to develop and nurture a passion in life, and doing stuff with other people – a book club, a spinning class, a choir – anything that involves direct interaction with others. And he mentioned that the British Government had appointed a junior minister whose lead brief is to address loneliness and social isolation, and that got people in Ireland talking about the need to introduce such a portfolio here, which makes sense when one considers that there are more people living on their own in Ireland now than at any other recorded period in history. Incredibly, studies suggest that being lonely is the equivalent of smoking 15 cigarettes a day, because loneliness will physically diminish and damage you, up to and including the point of expiration. A marble slab in a field. *Cremation and the Beach*. And that hit me right between the eyes, and offered another reminder about the benefits and importance of being engaged.

Goal setting, of course, can be a fraught business. Dreaming is part of my advocacy but if my two washing machine adventures have taught me anything it's that there's no harm whatsoever in setting short-term goals, albeit short-term goals which are so achievable, even easy, that should you mess up repeatedly and badly, you're still going to fall over the finish line. We may not all want to be remembered as some Eddie the Eagle-like character‡ who will do the odd tape-cutting gig at a new super-market long after the chat-show appearances and TV ads have dried up. But how many people reading this can include the word 'Olympian' in their Twitter bio? Eddie Edwards can, even if that Andy Warhol moment in his life impacted on millions watching from their sitting rooms 30 years ago. He may not have been an accomplished ski-jumper, but he still got to Calgary. He lived his dream. How many of us can say the same?

---

‡ Michael Edwards (born 5 December 1963), known as 'Eddie the Eagle', is an English ski-jumper and Olympian who in 1988 became the first competitor since 1928 to represent Great Britain in Olympic ski-jumping, finishing last in the 70-metre and 90-metre events. He held the British ski-jumping record from 1988 to 2001.

What's a realistic goal? Consider the following: it's late on a Sunday night, your inner monologue distracts you from *The Week in Politics* and you tell yourself, right, I'm going to run 10 miles every day this week. You may well cover that distance come Monday, you might even manage it on Tuesday but by Wednesday, with your arse cheeks set to consciously uncouple from the rest of your body, you're done for. By Thursday, you feel jaded and a bit useless, come Friday you'll order a takeaway, convincing yourself that white rice is a superfood and on Saturday you'll down three bottles of wine because you're depressed about not being able to run. You've probably forgotten that you did actually run 20 miles, and had you set a more realistic goal – say, three miles every day this week – you would have run 21 miles, you would feel fantastic about yourself, and, without giving too much thought to it, you would have covered most of a marathon distance without overdoing it, and you would be able to think about running 22 miles the following week.

Trying to get fit quick is as unrealistic as a get-rich-quick scheme. In a world where we want things more instantly than ever – be it 'likes' on a Facebook post, swiping one way or the other in the twenty-first-century dating game, or pressing 'order' for a pizza – it can be all too easy to forget that the goals worth striving for and the dreams worth pursuing can take time to realise. But goal-setting is what turns a 21-mile running week into 22, 23, 24 miles and onwards.

Consider the words of the great UCLA basketball coach, John Wooden:

'Take a moment and draw a circle around the following personal characteristics that you possess: confidence, poise, imagination, initiative, tolerance, humility, love, cheerfulness, faith, enthusiasm, courage, honesty, serenity. I hope you circled them all because all are within each of us. It is simply up to us to bring them out...

Perhaps you fret and think you can't make a difference in the way things are. Wrong. You can make the biggest difference of all. You can change yourself. And when you do that you become a very powerful and important force – namely, a good role model. I believe you can do more good by being good than in any other way.'[10]

The instantaneous life, the quick fix, is not that rewarding. I'm an alcoholic. I should know. Life, sometimes, has to be a struggle. Sacrifice is part and parcel of the dream delivery business. So when we choose to do something difficult and we have that moment of realisation, 'oww, this really hurts,' the chances are that if we can tolerate the pain on day one, then it won't be as bad on day two. Or, at the very least, you'll learn just how much pain you can tolerate, and you'll prepare yourself mentally to live with it and come out the other side of it. And one day, you'll be Rocky Balboa on top of that mountain, screaming 'Dragoooo!' That's why I'm up most mornings at six, downing a bowl of porridge with hazelnuts and honey, followed by an hour of spinning that will draw a puddle of sweat from me that even Christy Moore at his gigging peak would have been envious of.

For me, the difference between ordinary and extraordinary people is the 'extra'. They arrive five minutes earlier for training or stay on for extra practice, like Eric Cantona did during his time at Manchester United. And this captured the imagination of the 'Class of 92' – Ryan Giggs, Gary Neville, Paul Scholes, David Beckham, Nicky Butt – and it inspired them not only to greatness, but consistent greatness. The pursuit of perfection has led Brian Cody to 11 MacCarthy Cups and made Stephen Cluxton the most prominent Gaelic footballer of his generation. It's what makes Padraig Harrington so revered a figure in our sporting history. It's what has driven Rena Buckley to 18 All-Ireland senior titles, captaining Cork teams in both codes to the ultimate glory. It's what drives Katie Taylor to even greater heights in the ring. It's what makes Peter Freuchen such a hero of mine, and don't tell me that none of the above are or were dreamers.

How we learn to deal with failure and rejection is just as important as how we cope with achieving our goals and managing our own expectations. If things go wrong, I don't give a damn. And while failure does leave an impact, I've learned to redirect. Say I rang someone looking for sponsorship and I get a no, the rule I've established is that each 'no' has to be followed by at least five other phone calls. In a previous life – Enda 1.0 – being rejected like that would have been a crushing personal disappointment. I would have been left thinking what I'm trying to do is impossible, that I'm never going to get the message out there. But Enda 2.0 makes five more phone calls, and if they all end up with refusals, the bad news for me is that I'll have 25 more calls to make.

But at some stage in that process, I consciously change what I'm saying, my tone of voice and even the question I'm asking, and I eventually get lucky and that helps to keep things moving. Somebody asked me: 'How did you get that beautiful Renault van with your logo on it, the number and all the rest of it?'

I said, 'well, I just asked', and they go 'yeah right'. But what they don't know is that I had probably asked 20 other garages before some good fortune shone my way.

Roy Keane was told he was too small to become a professional footballer by people who supposedly knew better. He wrote a letter to Nottingham Forest, telling Brian Clough he had what it took to play at the highest level. Brian Clough saw enough in that letter to take a young lad away from Mayfield and watching *Neighbours* in the middle of the day, and the rest is soccer history. Why? Because Roy Keane asked. Because Roy Keane kept dreaming.

One of the ways in which you can measure your success is how well you can tolerate your failures, and how you learn from your failures. Former Tipperary hurling manager Michael Ryan, speaking in the wake of a National Hurling League defeat in Ennis, said that even when you lose, as a team, there are still positives to be elicited and learnings to be banked. There may well be losses, but there are never dead losses. And he's right. If something goes wrong and you learn from that, then there's still a gain at play, even if that gain isn't immediately evident, particularly on those days when you get your arse handed to you on a pitch or in a ring, or even in the office. And that's always stood me in good stead.

Mount Kilimanjaro is the prime example in my own experience of how to differentiate between individual disappointment and collective achievement. Fundamentally, the goal of the trip was to ask people to 'Share the Load', to raise money for Pieta House and to get more and more people talking about mental health and suicide. It wasn't about me getting to the summit with the washing machine. It wasn't about me at all. But the washing machine got to the summit, a lot of people's lives were forever altered by that trip, and a lot of people's lives will be saved thanks to the money we raised from that trip, so the goal was realised. In a bizarre way, for me, messing up was probably a fitting personal conclusion. It helped way more people, it helped raise way more money and I learned way more from it. I'd be lying if I said I wasn't disappointed about not reaching the summit, but it was the most humbling experience I ever had in my life to come to the realisation that this whole adventure was never about me. It was about a message; I was at peace before we were even on the flight home.

There was a video shot of our entire group the night after summit night and I've watched it more than a few times. I handed over an Irish flag to our Tanzanian friends as I wanted the next Irish group to come that way to see that some of their own had been there before them, and that a piece of home was waiting for them in a part of the world few of them would probably know too well upon arrival. I love the idea of transferring happiness through a piece of cloth six or twelve months down the line, so we had a handing over ceremony of the tricolour. That morning, the locals we'd come to call our friends, up and down that astounding mountain, performed their song about me – *Adu Machine Nguvu Kama Simba (The Washing Machine Man, Strong Like A Lion)*. I saw myself in that video, and – for someone who just 24 hours earlier had failed at something I'd been planning and training so long for – had pure joy on my face, dancing and jumping around with the group. The happiness and relief that came with the knowledge that everyone in our group was safe, that we'd raised a lot of money and achieved our goals – that made me smile. It made me grateful. It made me glad that I remain a dreamer.

I often use the diamond analogy when I'm giving a speech or speaking with a team. When you give a diamond to your partner and they hold it out against the light and everyone comments on how beautiful the bling is, that sparkle is created by its imperfections. That's all the mess-ups. All the things that went pear-shaped in the natural formation of that carbon is what gives a diamond its sparkle.

I like to think of the imperfections of my own life and all the imperfections in the adventures. Those elements have added value and sparkle to my life. Sure, I could do without the blisters, the diarrhoea, all the training and the sponsor-seeking phone calls, but all of those things are where the real value lies. That's what had me dancing in a tent in Tanzania a day after being told I needed to stop climbing unless *Cremation and the Beach* had bizarrely bolted up my running order.

Dreams are worth pursuing. I've lived out a few of mine. I'd like to think there's more to follow.

12

Accentuating the Positive

'There is nothing either good or bad, but thinking makes it so.'
William Shakespeare, *Hamlet*

When asked about writing a chapter on positivity, my initial thoughts on such a topic were ironically negative – go figure. I sat at home, pen and paper in tow, struggling to come up with something when I asked my daughter, Clodagh, for a few thoughts, but the manner in which I said it led her to reply: 'Well, the first thing you need to do is to be positive about it because if you ask anyone else about it in that tone of voice, you're not going to get anywhere with it!' And she was right. I'd infected my immediate environs with negativity and realised I'd have to change course and entirely reframe my perspective.

Most people who know me would, without hesitation, describe me as the most positive person they know. I have a really bad temper – like lava bubbling deep within Etna – but most of the time, I'd like to consider myself a bright and breezy type, and even when I'm not I convince myself and others around me that I'm in top form. Someone asked me how I remain so positive about pretty much everything, to which I replied: 'What's the alternative?' When you have truly experienced darkness, sadness and misery, when you've lived with depression and endured suicidal thoughts, anything that even resembles any of the aforementioned – well I just don't want any part of it anymore. Enda 2.0 is squarely focused on personal happiness and prioritising the value of mental health and positive well-being. And another reason I remain so positive is by viewing it as a choice. It's a route that's always available to me. By choosing positivity and embracing it so fully, I know that this particular choice can only make my life and the lives of those I know and love best even better.

My sentiments on positivity should not be considered as 'Enda-isms': it's not an idea I'd consider similar to carrying a washing machine up the world's tallest free-standing mountain. But it's a scientific and medical fact that if you're positive, that such an approach will deliver a positive impact on your life. There are numerous medical journals which state that your risk of heart disease is lessened if you're positively minded, as are your risks of anxiety and depression – and that's largely down to developing, retaining and working on one's positivity levels.

Business leaders and trainers will tell you that successful people tend to be happy, and that their happiness levels permeate through their work spaces: success, health and happiness make for a happy coming together, and that's why I'm so keen to hold onto my happiness and self-worth: because I know it's good for me and I know what it took for me to earn it. People want to be around forward-leaning, ideas-driven friends and colleagues – they want to spend time with high achievers, standard setters and agenda makers. Brian Clough, during an infamous TV interview with Don Revie, whom he briefly replaced at Leeds United, said: 'I want to be like me.' It's taken over half my life for me to find the safe harbour of self-worth. It's not a breakwater I'm in any rush to clear – nor do I intend to.

Actions followed by reactions tend to operate in cycles. For example, if you shout at someone, and this is something I've imparted to younger teachers over the years, you shouldn't be surprised when a student shouts back at you. As a teacher, you shouldn't be focusing on the 'neck' of the student to use their voice: you ought to concentrate on how you've chosen to use yours. It's human nature. The chances are that if you smile at someone, they're going to smile back. If you hit someone, the chances are you'll be hit in response.

Let me tell you about 'Mrs X' – not her actual name – but nonetheless a real person who grew up in my wife's home town and when we'd make a visit there, more often than not she would call in. The first thing she'd say whenever we were there was:

'Have you heard who's after dying? Yerra, he got a great send-off and he made for the most beautiful corpse. You'd swear looking at him that he was only having a rest in his good suit. And the four

TDs were there too. First back to the parish hall for the bowl of soup and all.'

And on and on she would go. This woman revelled in death and misery: a bit like the person who 'shushes' a room while the death notices are broadcast on local radio; she loved every post-flatlining detail, and I could never understand quite why. The haste which some of us devote to both obtaining negative information and then transmitting it elsewhere like a 'retweet' does not illustrate the best use of one's psyche. Ultimately, Mrs X's entire life revolved around misery and sadness until it reached the point where those who were closest to her simply but sadly withdrew from her life. They just couldn't take her unrelenting negativity any longer.

While some older newspaper readers like Mrs X still make with haste towards the memoriam pages, sport remains the first section I leaf through. Why? Because somebody always wins, it's generally people-centred and regularly driven by personality, there are guaranteed levels of drama and excitement, and its focus is not on misery – well, at least not the sport that I choose to read. It helps to take me to another place and it's a place I've always loved.

My sunny outlook was undoubtedly gifted to me by my parents, both Mullingar-born and bred, products of a rural upbringing rich in wisdom, be it honed from dealing with people, animals or both: they were always succinct and to the point. My mother had a great saying: 'Show me your friends and I'll show you your future', while my dad's one, maybe not quite as eloquent, goes like this: 'If you lie down with dogs, you'll get up with fleas!' But it's true. If you hang around with happy, positive people, that can only lead to a positive and productive impact on your own life. Tell me about it: the greatest moment of my life was Maeve accepting my marriage proposal. Without her, brandy and milk might have become my life-curtailing partner. When you're around the right people, good vibes invariably follow. You make better decisions not only for yourself but for those around you. We are masters of our own destiny. Shakespeare articulated mission statements for life through his characters: in essence, he tells us that thoughts direct actions and that actions determine reality. What those thoughts and actions are is entirely down to your mindset. To be or not to be really is the question.

The decline of religion in Ireland, and through much of old Christendom, has led it to be somewhat subsumed by pursuits such as mindfulness and yoga, to name but two. But set aside whatever your own pursuit may be and consider the following scientific fact: you're going to live longer and better, and be less susceptible to cancer and cardiac illness, by being positive in your life. So why not live your life more positively? Equally, why would you embrace the alternative given what that means for you and those you love? A 2005 project by the *Psychological Bulletin* tested 275,000 people, and of those tested the people who were successful were the people who were happy. Happiness, as the results indicated, directly impacted on your income and the nature of your relationships with people, be it those you live or work with. The University of Kansas conducted 'The Nun Study', in which they surveyed nuns aged between 17 and 35, and asked them to keep a written journal in which they measured the levels of positivity in their lives. Thirty to forty years later, by which time all of the surveyed nuns were in their senior years, the nuns who had survived were, by and large, those who had struck a consistently positive note in their respective diaries.

Positivity is a simple albeit powerful facet of life that a lot of us tend to either ignore for too long or never acknowledge the energy elicited from getting out of bed each and every day. As football pundit Gary Neville (up at 5 a.m. daily) puts it, attacking the time spent out of the scratcher, and making the utmost of your day. Your mindset not only dictates your physical being, but it determines your mentality on every possible front, at home, at work and at play.

On the walk between Belfast and Waterford, any time something went awry (and boy did they!), it became immediately apparent that we had to seek a remedy. If my feet were swollen, the positive element of such discomfort was an increase in views and likes on the Facebook page (which also meant more money for Pieta House) since a story without drama is hardly worth the telling. And the worse things got for me, the more it engaged the viewing public! For example, if I'd bought two pairs of boots, rotated them efficiently and started in Belfast by wearing a pair of boots that weren't going to be the source of multiple blisters, I'd probably have been in better physical shape, but where would the humour, drama and suffering have emerged from without the skin-peeling and bowel-emptying drama? I doubt if I'd have thought about a book without the speed bumps both life in general and the Pieta Challenges have thrown my way.

I know for a fact that I drive my family bananas with my positivity. They know, even before I open my mouth, when we sit down to talk about something, that I'm going to emphasise the positive because that impacts on my mindset, but it also impacts on them. But I'm equally aware that whenever they or others close to me have a crisis, they contact me because I've got a good ear but also because I always strive to find the best possible outcome from any situation. And the positives are always there: sometimes it takes a little longer to identify them and find them – but they're always there.

I approached the Kilimanjaro trek cognisant that I wasn't good with heights, was slightly claustrophobic and that I didn't like the darkness. But while there, I slept in a small tent in pitch darkness, sleeping on a stony surface above the cloud line. But Maeve, the singular positive influence of my life, was there, in that tent, alongside me. The first night that we unpacked the tent, Maeve returned inside to see that I'd produced a string of fairy lights with their own battery supply, and I hung them across the tent. So every night when we left the tent, predominantly to go to the toilet, we could instantly see our 'mountain lodge', lit up like a Christmas tree. Those lights cost me a Euro but you couldn't put a price on the smile creasing Maeve's face when she caught sight of them. Equally so, it calmed my nerves that I wasn't sleeping in complete darkness. For eight days, all of us slept in our clothes. We were dirty, we were smelly but, throughout that time, Maeve and I didn't have a cross word. I didn't think it was possible for us to get any closer or more intimate. But we did. We survived those eight days together without ever falling out. We also gave each other space and time when we needed it and on a personal basis, that elevated level of togetherness with my wife was the greatest single positive I brought home from Africa.

Emmanuel, the mountain guide who took particular care of me, is one of the most positive men I've ever met. And while this was the adventure of a lifetime for us, he goes up and down Kilimanjaro at least a dozen times annually. 'This is so hard, it's so difficult,' I said to him one morning, 'yet you smile every day. Why are you so happy?'

Emmanuel replied:

> 'Why? Because I am here. I am strong and healthy. I climb the mountain every day with a smile on my face because as I climb, I am thinking of my family. This mountain means that my family eat. This mountain means that my children receive an education.'

You couldn't be around Emmanuel and his colleagues without being positively affected by them. They were being paid very small money for hugely demanding physical labour yet they began every morning in song and dance – and I mean every morning. They laughed and smiled during the course of their work, but that positivity and affirming attitude is what makes the difference for any group operating in a challenging environment. It's what keeps them together, and I saw that same quality in our own team over eight draining days. The more they were squeezed, their response to pressure was to be happier, to be increasingly irreverent and to drop a dirty joke when the time demanded it. To be among Africans and Irish, walking together and smiling together, was stunningly educational, uplifting and inspiring. I've lived this experience and still can't quite believe, even now, that I was party to it. That I'd made this happen. The absolute joy of it.

Readjusting our minds to focus on gratitude opens our minds to the benefits of developing and sustaining a positive mindset. The morning we came down off Kilimanjaro, I said to myself that this was probably going to be my first and last trip to Africa, so we decided to go on a safari to the Arusha National Park. As we approached the park, the potholes grew bigger and bigger and we had to slow down just as we passed a Masai village. One house in particular really caught my eye. I could see the handprints of an entire family on the wattle-and-daub-type bricks they'd stacked in creating their home from mud, and it made me think about my beautiful home in Waterford.

Closer still to the park, I saw a family of four perched by a puddle. They were using a chipped enamel mug to scoop water from that puddle, drinking it, with the parents tending firstly to their children. The father, brandishing a spear, was at all times considering what he would need to do if a wild animal materialised from the bush. Yet their body language did not indicate a modicum of poverty or a scintilla of disillusionment: they beamed positivity while some of us on the bus were a little narked by its underperforming air conditioning. Talk about a contrast. I left Ireland as a middle-class teacher but I returned home as a rich man. Here I am, living in an electrified house with running water 24 hours a day, as opposed to walking four to five miles for water, never knowing what big cat might be lurking nearby, which is a daily reality for so many of the people we saw in Tanzania. The African people we encountered over those eight remarkable days were the most positive people I've ever met, and they've left a deep and lasting imprint, which I for one am grateful for.

How we begin is how we finish. Getting out of bed, determined to make the day ahead a positive experience both personally and for those we circulate amongst is the best option available to all of us. Why? Consider the alternative. Consider how your negative mindset and downbeat vocabulary can change the mood of a household or workspace. Then flip that coin and think how much better the glass half full option is. So that's why coffee, a smile, an upbeat conversation with Maeve over breakfast in bed and the foot-tapping strains of John Lee Hooker over the sound system is how I choose to start my day. I never want to start any day with a stumble on the ice. I don't want to be heading face first whenever I can avoid it. And I do all I can to stay on both feet each and every day.

I've had misery, heartbreak, death and loss in my life – they come to us all in varying degrees – and there's a great deal of those events which we have absolutely no control over. However, we can control how we respond to those events. Maeve saw that within me when it came to my relationship with alcohol. When I asked her why she'd never asked me to stop drinking and to cop the hell on for myself, she delivered a brilliant response:

> 'You are responsible for yourself. Your first duty in life is to your own health and happiness. You have to save yourself, Enda.'

And she was right. Improving my self-worth had to start with me. Maeve couldn't make that happen. This was a wheel that I and I alone was responsible for turning. Of course, there's a place for other forms of intervention – be it your wife, your mother (I, as a grown man with three kids, once drove to Naas for a hug from my mother following a panic attack) or a professional, but the only person who could get me out of my head and get my feelings in sync was me. Ultimately, I did get in sync, it takes work to stay there, but it's the most valuable and rewarding work I've ever remained committed to. And I've got to keep working on it. I value my happiness too much to drop that particular ball. But I never take it for granted.

The passing of my mother broke my heart and made me sad but in the interim, I've enjoyed a lot more time with my family, away from the house, enjoying their company and good humour. My mother's passing helped me to refocus my mind on how wonderful life should be and the significance of making the most of the 28,000 days most of us live on average.

If for some reason I depart for the great washing machine in the sky next week, next month or next year, I'll do so knowing I've had a fantastic life. I'll do so knowing I've done my best to control how I've reacted to the tough days I've had to face down during my life. Bobby McFerrin[§] nailed it: I've learned to be happy and not to worry. It's all in the mindset. And if you practice being happy long enough, more often than not, you might just end up with a smile on your face.

[§]   Bobby McFerrin was an American musician famous for the song 'Don't Worry, Be Happy'.

13

Mam

'For, in the final analysis, our most basic common link is that we all inhabit this small planet. We all breathe the same air. We all cherish our children's future. And we are all mortal.'[11]

President John Fitzgerald Kennedy

Theresa O'Doherty, husband to Tom, mother of my siblings, Fiona and Karl, and grandmother of nine, died on Wednesday, 16 May 2018.

My mam loved helping people. Her natural impulse was always to give and to reach out. For this and for so many more reasons, she was easy to love. Sitting by her bedside during the final days of her life was horrendous. It was sad, tragic, difficult and dark. But in the midst of it all, there was still time for levity, something the Irish can almost always be relied upon to produce even when clouds are at their darkest and most foreboding. We're good at letting the light in. It helps us to find a way out of grief or, at the very least, to tolerate the absence of someone we have forever known, loved and honoured.

Dad recalled going to Mass one Sunday with all of us walking up the main street in Naas when we noticed a particularly impoverished local family. And as we got nearer to them, my father grew quiet and gave me a little nudge. Anyway, after Mass, Dad told me that the father of the family had been wearing this beautiful, handmade suit, which he immediately recognised: it was his! Mam had decided that someone else needed that suit more than he did, and that was a typical thing for her to do. It came so naturally to her. That was my mother and that was how she lived her life.

No doubt to lift our spirits, and with perhaps an element of self-preservation at play given how draining that week was, and indeed the previous two years had been for him, Dad told us another story about a charity auction Mam had put on at the K Club (which hosted golf's Ryder Cup in 2006). Being the quiet type, my father stood at the back of the function room, and he was stood beside a man who was bidding for a camera. As the man grew hesitant about raising his bid, Dad persuaded him to keep raising his hand. 'That's a really good camera,' Dad assured him, 'It's a cine-camera. The case is good, the tripod is good, sure I've one at home myself.' Only it wasn't at home, as Dad later learned he had helped to successfully auction his own camera. That generosity of spirit occasionally came at a price for Dad!

We're the products of the homes we're born and reared in. I look like my father, but I sound like my mother and have a similar personality and outlook to hers. She was heavily invested in charity work and that interest initially stemmed from tragedy. Mam's best friend, Nora Burke, died from cancer and she spent her final days at Cork General Hospital alongside two patients with relatively trivial illnesses – tonsillitis and appendicitis, I think. So Nora's family had to mourn and say goodbye to a loved one in this sort of environment – and my mother thought that this was wrong. She founded a committee and began fundraising, and by the late 1980s she'd managed to raise £3.5 million through American tea parties, draws, dinner dances, etc. Our house on the Sallins Road in Naas was always heavily populated by collection cans, t-shirts and posters, and we were routinely dragged to charity event after charity event, something which, in time, would prove beneficial when it came to my own cajoling and fundraising escapades. The local newspaper ran a lovely article about my mother's endeavours under the most apt of headlines, 'A Generous Impulse'. We were all so proud of what Mam did and the work she was so committed to and enthused by.

Mam was just relentless. She would develop tunnel vision once she identified a project or worthy cause and developed a clear goal. She devoted herself fully to fulfilling that objective. All or nothing, that was Theresa O'Doherty. And it's only occurred to me in recent years that so much of who we are as adults and what we choose to do in adulthood stems from our most prominent early influences. She was a big fan of President John F. Kennedy, and like so many Irish households in the 1960s and 70s, we had pictures of the 35th American President hanging proudly at home, meaning yes, more than one! She regularly recalled two JFK quotes to us, starting with his inauguration call, 'Ask not what your country can do for you, ask what you can do for your country'. Mam firmly believed that community was formed and consolidated by action rather than complaint, and that doing something could make a difference. She lived her life by that maxim. She also used to cite a Bible verse JFK regularly referenced at the end of a day in which us three smallies might have spent a good portion of time tearing strips off each other: 'never let the sun go down on your anger.' That principle is upheld in my own home today. Resolution is always the end goal. After all, tomorrow could be the last day. She really was a mighty woman. An amazing woman.

Mam played cello, viola, violin and piano to Grade 8 and turned down the opportunity of joining the RTÉ Symphony Orchestra to make a life and a family with my father. 'I could have been in Prague or Vienna,' she would wistfully declare when the mood struck her. 'But I chose nappies in Kildare instead!'

When I was 15, while most of my friends wanted to be footballers Lou Macari or Steve Heighway, I wanted to be my mother. There was no way I could say that at the time because I'd have been slaughtered. Her unlimited kindness was what I most admired about Mam, and it's a facet I've attempted to incorporate into my own life. She had a huge social circle, a family devoted to her, was a great public speaker and an inspiration to so many people. For me, my mother's kindness defined her. She eked something out of every day until cancer made its unwelcome intrusion. She just loved life and she loved giving.

Every day, week and month of the 73 healthy years Mam could readily recall and revisit was full of positive things. As Dad said one night in the hospital:

'Sometimes it could be exhausting living with your mother. She knew everybody, talked to everyone, was involved in everything and helped everyone. And there was no end to it with her.'

Now, my mam could have lived to 90 or 95; however if she'd lived for that long without packing in what she did before falling ill at 73 and dying at 75, but opted just to sit in an armchair and wonder when the next meal was due, I'd not have wanted that for her. That, to me, is not living. That's existing. The chronology of her lifespan might be considered below average for norms in Western society, but there was nothing average about my mother and the way in which she lived her life. She may not have played in a symphony orchestra but she lived her life symphonically. She pursued a greater purpose in everything she did: in being the best parent and spouse she could be, through her countless friendships and many charitable pursuits. Theresa was a thoroughly interesting woman. She drew every drop out of every day and I know that's rubbed off on me. I'll be forever grateful for that. Filling your life is surely the best way to live your life, and we buried Mam knowing that she had completely filled hers. We all drew great comfort from that, and it'll mean even more in the years to come.

Six months before she died, before cancer robbed Mam of her lucidity and ability to communicate, I visited her at home and told her straight out why I loved her and how much I loved her. It was akin to entering a confessional. I told her about the bad things I'd done too. Everything. As a kid, my parents used to call me 'Béal Mór' (Big Mouth): growing up, Mam spoke predominantly in Irish to me and that fostered a deep love within me for the language. My deep love of alcohol was a devotion of an altogether more damaging kind for both myself and my family, for they were the collateral damage caught up in my twister – even unwittingly from their perspectives – Mam in particular.

Dad has always been terrified of drink. His mother was an alcoholic and she died in August 1968, the month that I was born. He had seen at first hand what alcohol could reduce a family to and I've rarely returned home as an adult without being reminded of the pain he'd endured when he lost his mother. Indeed, he mentions it to me practically every time we talk. My grandmother had a pub, not the greatest business for an alcoholic to have, and Dad was left permanently scarred by how her alcoholism had impacted on his upbringing. I don't think either Mam or Dad knew the extent of my problem because, like so many alcoholics, I was very calculated. I might sit at the dinner table and have a glass of wine, when most of it was vodka. They'd see me having two glasses of wine, which would be considered responsible drinking, when in truth I'd probably just downed a half-pint of vodka. I can't recall Mam ever saying anything directly to me about it. We never had the big chat about booze – maybe because Dad would speak so openly and regularly about alcoholism, she felt he had it covered. But the more Dad said about drink, the more of a thirst it put on me.

I was pig-headed enough to believe that alcohol wouldn't colonise me and that I would remain its lord and master. Nothing could have been further from the truth, and Dad could see that, as plain as day. But I do believe that one of the things that has given my father most happiness in his 70s, and now into his 80s, is that I've not touched a drop for over 10 years. Maybe he'd had that conversation with Mam about what he could see in me while I was drinking and what I've been like since I stopped drinking. I can't answer that. But Dad has told me time and time again how pleased he is to see me happy, healthy and sober, and what that has meant to him. I know that Mam knew I was in a much better place over the last 11 years of her life, and I hope that made her feel good too. The 'Black Sheep', as Dad still addresses me whenever I appear back home at the front door, is doing just fine nowadays.

Incidentally, that branding remained long after I'd emerged from the brandy bottle and it's a nickname I've grown to love. Mam and Dad were both incredibly forgiving people, and full of good intentions.

There was a lot of sadness, pain and hurt at Mam's funeral Mass, but I began my eulogy by stating: 'My name is Enda, and I was, by far, Theresa's favourite child!' And the place erupted as tears turned to laughter. Again, tapping into humour made everyone feel a little better, myself included. I spoke about how much she packed into her life, including a term as President of the Soroptimists International for Great Britain and Ireland, who work to educate and empower women and girls. She shone like the star we all knew she was when she became national president. When she entered a room, everyone knew it and by the time she left that same room, everyone in there had made a friend for life just by meeting her.

She was obsessed with the British royal family – which was a source of bemusement to me – JFK and everything to do with Switzerland, where Karl was conceived. She was a great fundraiser, a tremendous socialiser but a terrible cook: Mam was a dab hand at burning the arse out of a saucepan, and I just assumed that this was something all mothers did! Nobody's perfect, but my goodness Mam gave life the best possible shot. She really did.

Mam has left behind an incredible legacy. The manner in which she reached out and positively impacted upon so many lives is an example that I will always strive to live by. That incredible kindness. That generous impulse. This grateful son has much to be proud of.

14

Advice to Enda (Aged 21)

'You have been formed of three parts – body, breath, and mind. Of these, the first two are yours insofar as they are only in your care. The third alone is yours.'

Marcus Aurelius, *Meditations*

Were I to reach the magical 88mph in Doc Brown's DeLorean and revisit my past to seek out my 21-year-old self, I'm not sure he'd have been on for a heart-to-heart, as tying him down for longer than a few minutes would surely prove problematic. After all, there was too much partying to be done!

Example: Towards the end of another hectic night's drinking in college – I was also on a course of antibiotics at the time – I caught sight of a large pampas bush outside the house I was nominally staying in and clambered into its 'inviting' thicket. Despite my feet protruding out of the bush, as far as I was concerned, I'd found my bed for the night. It really is amazing how an excess of alcohol rationalises the most idiotic of thoughts. The girls whom I was meant to be staying with returned home shortly after I'd 'bunked up', saw my feet dangling out of the bush and 'knocked' on my shoes, explaining that I was only 20 yards from a house and the logic of a warm, indoor bed. But I was very angry with them for disturbing me: I couldn't understand what they were doing in my 'room' and why they'd disrupted the great sleep that I'd been having. So I have to wonder what good, if any, would have been elicited from a sit-down chat with my younger, brandy-soaked incarnation. He'd probably have told me to lighten up, have a pint and hop into the pampas for a body-warming bout of spooning!

Since there can't be many among us who wouldn't have terminated a young Adolf Hitler busily tinting postcards in Vienna, there's always a chance that my younger self might have taken on board some of what I would present to him as worthwhile and sustainable life options. Firstly, I'd tell him to 'Get Up Earlier'. When you get up early, at least in my experience, you tend to sleep better and when you sleep better, tomorrow's a better day already. I'm up most mornings nowadays between 5 a.m. and 5.15, and that's a particular joy in the summer, living as I do within proximity of the River Suir as it flows around the islanded Waterford Castle. In addition to my early morning coffee with Maeve, I read, I watch, I listen and I work out. I'll have my son dropped to work and might meet someone else for a chat or another coffee before most people are out of the scratcher to go to work. It's a brilliant time of the day, a window that I've carved out not only for myself, but with Maeve too. It fuels me, it engages me and it energises me, and that's all well before 9 a.m. By then, I've already put down a brilliant day before clocking in. I know we need more sleep when we're younger, and I know it's a time in our lives when we ought to let the hair down and really live, but I do wish I'd gotten up earlier during my 20s and 30s. Time is such a precious commodity, and enriching time remains a concept largely lost on the young. Putting it to good use is the best way of making each and every day count. Because every day ought to matter.

I also wish I'd given away more rather than accumulating stuff the way I did. If you're Augustus Gloop-like once a cookie jar opens, with your sole focus on grabbing as many goodies as you can, more often than not you just end up with crumbs and disappointment. The happiest experiences that I've had in my life have involved giving things away. And as the years pass by, I find myself giving away more and more. Thankfully, the speaking circuit has been going well for me these past few years and I've made some decent money out of it, but I've had times in my life when I've made a lot of money and felt miserable while I've had phases when I've not had much spare cash yet I've been very happy. Life is odd and beautiful like that and I guess that's why we can never make complete sense of it all of the time.

Investing in yourself was a realisation Maeve and I arrived at while perched at our front door, observing a skip full of household detritus we'd filled over the guts of a day, stacked with as much stuff as we could wedge into it. Being Irish of course, the skip had to have makeshift sides erected down both lengths to offload all those bits and bobs that we no longer needed. I hammered and hacked away at a bookshelf from which our elevated skip sides were created, and it did the job nicely. Maeve vividly remembered the day we had bought that bookshelf. This was something we'd saved money for, an object which was going to make us happy, something we lodged in our sitting room and filled with books, a great many of which we never read. And as we surveyed our handiwork, the bookshelf in particular, we both agreed that largescale investments in objects no longer made much sense to us: that we needed to invest in ourselves, prioritise our health and maximise our life experiences because, at the end of the day, that's all you have.

When you're on your deathbed, I suspect you'll not evaluate your life by how many bookshelves you have, how many pints you downed or your number of Facebook 'friends', a great many of whom you probably haven't shared a spoken 'hello' with during any given 12-month period. What's in your heart, what's in your head and who's with you is all that really matters, and that's why the skip and the bookshelf was such a note-worthy moment. It represented the moment that we both decided to do things differently and to recognise that the best investment we'd ever made in life was in each other and our children. I just wish this realisa-tion had come a little sooner, yet I'm just as grateful for that moment of revelation, sat on our front step, gazing at an iron jaw full of dusty, discarded domesticity.

The penny jar a lot of us keep at home may not have too much in it on day one, but in six to seven years' time, those pennies will pile up and literally amount to something. Together, all of those coins have accu-mulated value, which brings to mind something else I'd have told my 21-year-old self: be aware of what pennies you collect. If you think about 'health pennies', you might subconsciously have that vodka or drag on a cigarette, but if you do consume enough of both, you're putting negative health pennies into a jar. Accumulate enough of those bad pennies and you're going a long way towards sclerosis of the liver or even lung cancer.

A bad relationship can inject psychological toxins into not only both parties, but catalyse a blast radius which extends beyond the threshold of your home. And again, the notion of a relationship or a marriage falling into disrepair represents an accumulation of these bad pennies that fill the jar in the worst possible way, eroding value in life, sometimes with devastating consequences. Taking that into account, I'm very mindful of trying to collect positive pennies and on those occasions when I was required to say a few words at a family gathering, I used to talk about 'laethanta órga' – the golden days – and for me, golden days are those occasions when you can look back, even on your worst day, and feel a rush from recalling it. A chat. A song. A laugh. All positive pennies in the jar. And if I could tell 21-year-old Enda about accumulating memories, I'd urge him to make as many good memories as he can, to listen to those looking out for him and to take on board things that are going to help him, long beyond those hazy nights when a pampas bush looked like a decent sleeping arrangement. Appreciate the value in yourself and those around you. Pile those pennies good and high!

I'd also urge him to plan more. Sometimes in our younger years, we just let life happen, and I say that without trying to be too OTT on the OCD front. By planning, we tend to develop greater efficiency levels and get the best out of ourselves at whatever task we've chosen to busy ourselves with. I regularly have students talking to me in full exam post-mortem mode, talking about everything they felt just went wrong or, in a sporting scenario, have a defender coming into a dressing room talking about the opposition's massive centre-forward, and it's amazing how good a lot of us are at analysing what goes pear-shaped in life or in sport: more negative penny gathering. What we're not so good at is pre-mortem, at planning for what we hope we can avoid materialising. Something else that I feel most of us naturally struggle at is assessing, even accepting, that there are times when we do something well, and that it's okay to feel good, even great, about such moments. We appear to have little trouble with magnifying negativity and, in a manner similar to how we Irish struggle with compliments and positive feedback, socially we're still falling down when it comes to magnifying and basking in positivity. And we can feel good without our egotism alienating or belittling others. The path to happiness has to and must begin with the self: Maeve told me that and Maeve was right. We can learn lessons from things we didn't do as well in the past and then endeavour to do better in the future. As Alfred (Michael Caine) tells Bruce Wayne (Christian Bale) while Wayne Manor went up in flames during *Batman Begins*: 'Why do we fall, sir? So that we can learn to pick ourselves up.' Life gets a whole lot easier when you're off your haunches.

Be your own hero. We should allow ourselves permission to dream about becoming the best version of ourselves. Having worked with successful people and sports teams, I can tell you that they're exactly the same as you or me. But what may distinguish them from the pack rests in how their dreams are matched by actions. So I would tell my younger self that if I'd like to have my own business, yes, it mightn't work out, but it definitely won't work out if you don't take action.

A piece of body ink I once saw sprung to mind when I thought about what I'd like to tell my wet-behind-the-ears, hungover incarnation: '*Every day do something that others won't, then one day achieve something that others can't.*' Carrying a washing machine from Belfast to Waterford and up (most of) Kilimanjaro is something that 99 per cent of people simply wouldn't countenance from a physical or mental perspective. And even if I didn't personally get that Beko to the summit, the machine got there. I learned the value of 'Sharing the Load' and it made me a better person. I drew down the 'guaranteed dividend' that John Wooden extolled during his extraordinary college basketball career.

> 'I believe one of the big lessons of sports for dedicated individuals and teams is that it shows us how hard work, and I mean *hard* work, does pay dividends. The dividend is not *necessarily* in outscoring an opponent. The guaranteed dividend is the complete peace of mind gained in knowing you did everything within your power, physically, mentally and emotionally, to bring forth your full potential. I see the same self-satisfaction occurring in every area of our lives when we strive mightily to do our best, whether it's working in a business or community or raising a family. The great satisfaction that comes from trying to do your best is the guaranteed dividend.'[12]

The thinking of something is so often worse than its doing. Dream but then act. Don't become a prisoner of your worst fear. Use fear as a trigger for action. Dare to be an advocate for your ambitions. Become that better angel. Spread those wings. Be open to more directions in life. And just do it. It makes the journey so much better. Older me knows that now. I've learned and I've won, and that feels great.

There's so much joy to be gained in helping others, and that's something I appreciate now in a manner I could simply never have fathomed as a 21-year-old. When I was younger, I regularly wondered what on Earth motivated anyone to be a scout leader or a juvenile soccer coach. Had those people no lives of their own? Had they nothing better to do? But now as a more socially aware adult than I was - way back at a time in my life when I hadn't accumulated all those positive and negative pennies that led to Enda 2.0 - helping others is the greatest single pursuit I can think of. It's incredible therapy. It boosts self-worth. It leads to new friendships. There's a myriad of reasons to reach out and help other people, and if I'd done so 25 years earlier, I can only imagine the fulfilment and contentment I'd have gained from living like that.

But when I was 21, I just didn't have the wisdom to take such a path. I recently told Maeve I wished I'd been doing this sort of work for years.

> 'But you couldn't have done what you've done in the last few years without embarking on your own journey and all that you've gone through.'

Standing in front of a class, speaking for six hours a day, five days a week for over 20 years allows me to stand comfortably in front of people and articulate, explain, empathise and entertain, I hope.

Read more. To my shame, while I was in college, I was always the fella who made a beeline for the summary. I never read a book from cover to cover in those years – page seven was generally where my interest died – whereas now I'm a sponge for learning. I can't get enough stuff between my ears nowadays, which fills me with so much regret when I consider that in a 20-year spell, the only book I read was *The Van* by Roddy Doyle while on honeymoon. But as I've begun to reverse that trend in recent years, reading has provided me with so much additional insight; it's catalysed so many ideas that I really wished I'd put my college years and the 15 that followed to much better use from that perspective. Opening books has opened doors for me and I've a lot of work yet to do on that front.

Embrace the outdoors. Training with the washing machine forced me to get out and it opened my eyes to the power of sunlight and the glory of nature. Hiking up alongside Mahon Falls and standing over Coumshingaun Lake in the Comeragh Mountains, with the patchwork of mid-Waterford fields and the stunning Copper Coast beneath me, I came to appreciate the true beauty of this place which has become my adult home. For years and years, I'd been completely blind to the beauty of the county I lived in. To think I'd spend thousands to travel abroad to savour mountains, valleys and seas, yet all of the above is just a few minutes from my house by car. Oh Waterford, what a beauty she is.

Be aware of what lying leads to. Everyone lies. To their parents, their spouses, their friends – granted to varying degrees – but everyone at some stage in their lives lies, be they grave or white. I would say to my 21-year-old self: be aware of lies. Be aware of the power of your words. For me, the biggest lies I ever told were to myself:

> 'You're not drinking too much. You're grand. Life is fine. Keep going. Ignore the successive nights of boozing.'

How wrong I was. The one person I wish I'd been more honest with was me. I should have acknowledged what was wrong a lot earlier than I did and that brings me back to the negative pennies in the jar. By lying to myself, I paid a long-term price. Twenty-one-year-old me didn't think about the concept of alcoholism. I was too busy enjoying myself, having the time of my life. I was working as a tour guide in Glendalough and I recited the following both in English and French. I still can:

> 'The valley of the two lakes, sometimes sombre and always beautiful. Here in the sixth century, Saint Kevin founded what later became known as St Kevin's monastic city. The round tower is an incredible 33 metres in height and stands on a one-metre foundation. The carved windows face the cardinal points of north, south, east and west. In 1872, the roof of the cathedral was struck by lightning.'

The guiding gig kept me busy for six months each over two successive summers without ever getting too introspective about all the levels of alcohol I was imbibing but the work undoubtedly influenced my teaching and public speaking styles, so there were some long-term benefits too.

Travel more. Laugh more. Learn more and consider the words of Marcus Aurelius: 'A person's worth is measured by the worth of what he values.'

Value your physical health. Value your mental health. Value the people you love. Value good times and don't forget to value yourself. If you want good things to happen, then believe in good things, invest in good things and never give up on them. Invest as much as you can in each day and those positive pennies will happily heap up. *Carpe diem* indeed.

15

Stress – Our Constant Companion

'I've seen the marlin mate and know about that. So I leave that out. I've seen a school (or pod) of more than fifty sperm whales in that same stretch of water and once harpooned one nearly sixty feet in length and lost him. So I left that out. All the stories I know from the fishing village I leave out. But the knowledge is what makes the underwater part of the iceberg.'[13]

Ernest Hemingway

Experiencing stress can sometimes lead to discovering the obvious. Christopher Columbus was trying to find the Spice Islands when he ran into America, yet history has widely described that collision with a continent as a 'discovery'. The obvious is sometimes right in front of us, and from time to time I'd wager we've all walked right into the blindingly opaque, and this readily applies when it comes to stress – and how to manage it.

Technically, the only person who has no stress is someone lying on a slab on a mortuary, and while we all know that day will come to us all, the path between now and then shouldn't involve an overwhelming, near suffocating sense of pressure, which, in itself, could shorten the gap between now and the last rites.

But stress in itself is absolutely vital. Players need a coach to highlight elements and techniques that they in turn can incorporate into their game to become better players. Even the most seasoned actor, who may well have a wing at home devoted to awards and garlands, will recognise the need to take notes from a director.

Dave Alred, the coach who moulded Jonny Wilkinson into the greatest goal-kicking machine of his rugby-playing generation, articulates the stress management techniques of elite athletes in *The Pressure Principle* – a book which any coach operating at any level of sport would do well to have on his book shelf. He is an advocate of the 'little and often' approach to preparing for a major challenge, be it on the sporting front or in day-to-day life. He writes:

> 'During the 2003 Rugby World Cup campaign with England, the backs would do a ten-to-fifteen-minute kicking and catching practice at the end of each training session, which could be twice a day. These short, sharp and intense bouts of practice, in which the players would be pushed to the margins of their ability, are the kind of blueprint you could take into your own life. Many people have extremely busy work and family lives, but if you could fit in just half an hour at the end of your working day, every day, be it to practice on the piano or work on that 5k run, then, provided it is an intense session, you can reap the benefits from even a small amount of regular time in the ugly zone.'[14]

He's right. Whether you're planning to get fit enough to compete at Ironman level, carry a washing machine up Kilimanjaro or if you're preparing for a job interview, you have to be prepared to spend time in the ugly zone and acknowledge the fact that stress is part of every facet of life. It's how we deal with it that defines us.

A presentation I regularly make to different workforces in different companies involves a series of slides, the second of which I like to describe as the 'blue screen of death'. The text 'Hard Disk Error' is emblazoned across the screen, a reality which practically any of us who've sat in front of a screen have experienced, doubly aggravating when we've not been clicking the 'Save' button on a regular basis in the hour or so before computerised Armageddon strikes. In reality, my computer is fine – I've Photoshopped this into my presentation – but at that moment, no one in the hotel room hired for the event is aware of this contrived fakery, apart from yours truly that is. So I pretend to be stressed and overwhelmed by this embarrassing 'failure,' but what amazes me each and every time I do this, is how many people come forward to help and try to alleviate my stress.

It's amazing how, despite the many stresses we have in our lives individually, we're still prepared to enter someone else's ugly zone and take on their stress too. The sympathy I've received when the blue screen emerges has been warm, generous and sincere. Thankfully, practically everyone sees the funny side of the story when the blue screen evaporates and the slideshow clicks on. People find themselves laughing at how they reacted to my supposed lack of organisation. But the greater point I try to make at that moment is that you may well have enough stress to deal with in your own life as it is: it's perfectly fine to not go looking for anyone else's.

'You Stress' is something I place great stock in. It's a positive stress which promotes growth and allows us to realise our goals. It's that injection of fuel which allows us to rise above the norm. Bad stress contributes to hair loss, weight gain, hypertension, anxiety, sleep disorder, cancer and a million other things. But good stress can help you achieve your ambition. If you can perceive a small amount of stress as a practical ally, it can significantly increase your concentration levels. It doesn't have to be a constant imp on one shoulder, whispering demotivation.

For example, if I'm doing a one-on-one coaching workshop I'll often ask the person I'm sat with how much time has elapsed since the session began, and typically they'll be out by 50 per cent! Someone I once sat with for three hours thought only an hour and ten minutes had elapsed; his concentration levels had increased so much by virtue of my coaching a little bit of 'good' stress that time appeared to fly by during our session.

A lot of stress can stem from the negative narrative which we create for ourselves. I often ask people to keep a diary for a week and to take note of every negative internal thought or outward utterance, and then read back through those comments at the end of the week. If anyone else in our lives spoke to us the way we do to ourselves, you'd never have anything to do with them. You'd avoid them like the plague!

Yet think about the things we've all said, bleary eyed, in front of a mirror, brushing our teeth at the start or indeed the end of the working week. 'Jesus, look at the belly on you. Your hair is falling out. You'll never get those suit trousers on for the wedding. You've nothing in the bank.' We say these things to ourselves over and over, time and time again. We've normalised bad stress. In as much as most of us are uncomfortable with people heaping praise in our direction – which I feel is a universal sentiment and not specifically intrinsic to the Irish – we're also uncomfortable with the idea of being outwardly confident. For example, Bill Cullen's 4-a.m. starts and telling himself aloud 'I am terrific' to his reflection every morning has earned him condescension and mockery in some quarters. Now I'll take being somewhat confident and feeling a little better about myself each and every time over self-flagellation, ergo increasing our own stress levels.

Perhaps that flagellation is something we use to avoid stepping outside of our own comfort zone. It grimly keeps us in check, like a giant elastic band clung to our midriffs, a self-defeating mechanism which we've determined will drag us back to the point that we've determined will be our limit, the point in life we'll never leap beyond. That's the moment you give up on a dream. All that's left thereafter is the slow punctured spin to the funeral home.

During one of my presentations, I display the six worst things that have ever been said to me. Three of them include:

1. Well now, you're putting on weight, aren't you?
2. God, your wife's too good-looking for you.
3. Your hairline is retreating quicker than your average French infantry battalion.

These are really nasty, personal things that have been said to me over the years. And as they appear on the screen behind me, I've regularly seen people sitting in the function room that's my theatre for a couple of hours visibly recoiling. I see the questioning look across many a face perched just a few yards from me wondering who on Earth has said this to me. And then up pops the next slide, which reveals the perpetrator's identity. It's me. Enda the self-flagellator.

Stress, far too regularly, stems from our own negative disposition. And we can programme ourselves into wearing that thick elastic band and opting for the slow puncture through life. But we can handbrake turn our way out of that and turn the car in the opposite direction. We can tell ourselves positive messages. We can teach ourselves to see things differently. We can keep on dreaming.

Famed UCLA coach John Wooden, as he did in so many ways, addressed that maxim succinctly:

'Early on I came to believe that you should learn as if you were going to live forever, and live as if you were going to die tomorrow. What does this mean? In the simplest way, I would explain it like this. Always be learning, acquiring knowledge and seeking wisdom in a sense that you are immortal and that you will need much knowledge and wisdom for that long journey ahead. Know when you are through learning, you are through. But I want to live that life as if I were going to die tomorrow: with relish, immediacy, and the right priorities. I also will not waste even a minute.'[15]

It is possible to see things differently. For years, I dealt with my stress by diving into a bottle. My elastic band of self-restraint was soaked in brandy. My only means of escaping stress or any difficulty I had was to completely and utterly fail to acknowledge my stress. Sure why bother with that when I could lace my system with vodka or brandy? I didn't have a huge difficulty in dealing with stress because I thought I was able to bury it, suppress it, make it disappear. But if you bury stress deep enough, it's just like a truffle in the ground. All it's going to do is grow. You might think you've put it to sleep. But if you've surrounded it with soil, all you've done is given your stress a chance to seed, sprout and re-emerge. And it's going to come back bigger and bite you in the arse. Using avoidance or attempting to ignore the source of one's stress is not stress management. Being proactive and dealing with your problems gives you a chance to cut free from that elastic loop. Alcohol is never proactive. Never.

One of the techniques I use in seminars to illustrate stress is to manifest it. A typical scenario would involve my telling a group of 100 or 150 people that I'm going to randomly pick one of them by a touch on the shoulder and whoever is selected will have to come to the front of the room and sing 'Happy Birthday'. I'd also play dramatic music when making this declaration and every time I do this I can feel the tension building among the group. Arms are folded. Legs are crossed. Heads are lowered. Others stare right up at me, adopting a 'come on, I dare you' stance. I can sense people, all around me, getting wound up. My action is making them experience stress. When I tell them that no one is actually going to have to sing and that I've just been winding them up, the mood changes again. When I've asked groups about how many of them thought that they, individually, would be asked to sing 'Happy Birthday', I usually get a 90 per cent show of hands, which suggests to me that 90 per cent of those in front of me are expecting that 'oh crap' moment. 'He's going to pick me. This is my worst nightmare.'

A typical reflection I offer in such a scenario generally goes something like this:

'Most of you just experienced unexpected stress in a matter of moments. Your heart rate probably went up. You may even have felt nauseous. The idea of coming up here and singing in front of everybody felt horrendously difficult. And it made you behave differently. You saw. You felt. You believed. We perceive stress in terms of how it will individually impact upon us. I would have found times in the past when I felt tension in my shoulders when sat in front of a laptop, when my breathing was rapid, when I wasn't sleeping well: that was probably a physical manifestation of stress in my life. And if you have those physical manifestations, the chances are that mental symptoms will become evident: irritability, intolerance, an inability to concentrate, becoming frustrated over small matters and so on. Stress is always there but it's not what happens to us that's important – it's our response to it, and because it's *our* response we can choose how to respond. Let me give you an example of that, a pretty incredible example, I feel, but one certainly worth sharing with you.

Back in 1987, I was flying back from Austria – I'd won a competition to speak on human rights over there – and I was sat alongside an elderly man, and I couldn't help noticing his puckered skin. It looked like he'd gone through some serious trauma and the wound looked quite old. So we're sitting there on the runway in Vienna, waiting for the plane to taxi, and I couldn't help but ask him about the wound. And what he told me was life-changing. "I'm a Holocaust survivor," he said. "My wife and I haven't visited Austria since the Second World War – and would you believe it, I met her in Auschwitz. And this scar of mine? Let me tell you how I got that. The day the camp was liberated by the Americans, I found a knife and I cut the SS branding from my arm. I was a commodity to the Nazis, something to experiment with. They didn't see me or anyone else they branded in the camps as human beings. And I wanted to live the rest of my life with my scar, rather than their hateful mark."

After the war ended, he and his wife left Europe for America, had their children there and had managed to rebuild their lives and find happiness again. And I was absolutely dumbstruck. It was an amazing story. And I said to him: "What you went through would be enough to destroy most people for life." To which he replied: "For me, it was a simple choice. And I chose to be happy. I told myself that I remained master of my own destiny. The Nazis hadn't taken that from me. They never took away my choice – and I chose to be happy. And it was the best choice I ever made – and I've had a wonderful life." It was the most incredible conversation. It would have been so easy and quite logical for that man's life to have become one filled with hate and sadness but he chose a different response. And those of us who've never lived through such a nightmare should consider the choices that he made in the face of such trauma when it comes to how we deal with and manage our own stresses. Because we always have a choice. We always have a choice. And we can choose happiness.'

Recalling that conversation now, it still makes the hairs stand on the back of my neck.

***

Choices. We all have them. That initial thought when you get out of bed in the morning can define not only your day, but that of the person in bed alongside you, the kids down the hall and, of course, your work colleagues. Working on making that first thought in the morning a positive one, to view the day ahead as a challenge rather than a chore, takes more practice for some than others. But it's worth the effort. And as part of that 'can-do' regime, when you take the time to reflect on what you want to do better without discarding what you already do well, how you alleviate and manage your stress levels is something we're all readily capable of.

I'm a long-time advocate of the following three-step approach and there are times I've often thought about how blindingly obvious these steps are. But one of the great Western philosophers of the 1980s couldn't have been more on the nose when he declared: 'Life moves pretty fast. If you don't stop and look around once in a while, you could miss it.' How right Ferris Bueller was!

1. Identify what's stressing you and find ways of diluting it, diffusing it, even eliminating it. For example, here's what I do when it comes to any day I wake up knowing I'll be on the road after school to speak at a seminar. I'll have my suit at the end of the bed the night before, my socks in one shoe and my jocks in the other. My watch is positioned beside my shoes. The wallet is left in the car (but not in plain sight folks!) to avoid the last minute 'Jesus Christ' outbursts that would have earned us all lines or worse back in our school days. I've filled the

car the night before; I never ever pull in on the day of a decent drive for fuel. It's just not how I roll! The tank is full in the yard and the car is facing out of the yard. Any day I'm setting off to tell students, a work force or a sports team about making every single step taken forward and progressive, I'm damned if I'm making my first journey anywhere that particular day in reverse gear. My lunch is on the passenger seat. All of my presentation equipment is in the boot. All these steps I've outlined alleviate my stress on such days. The hours before the working day begins shouldn't be the 'First Reading from the Book of Stress According to Enda'. Whenever I have a speaking engagement, I want and need to get there calmly. I want the people I'm speaking with (but never to) to hear me at my best. It's just like the working stage actor who makes no distinction between a Wednesday matinee audience and a heaving Saturday night crowd.

2. We can change how we respond to stress. Now, initially this might feel like trying to change an ocean liner's course when locked in a canal with a bag of concrete strapped to your back (or hey, maybe even a washing machine!) but again, this all comes down to choices and what we choose to do with those choices. And this may involve learning a new coping technique when it comes to handling stress. And, again, this can take time.

However, it can also represent something as simple as counting to 10 before replying to a comment uttered during a stressful moment, and taking the time to recognise that the frontal lobe of the left hemisphere of the brain is where speech and, more importantly in this instance, comprehension literally stems from. If angels fear to tread in certain areas, bearing in mind they can fly out of trouble, why walk barefooted into a briar patch? So do what Ferris Bueller advised. Stop and look around. Avoid fight and sidestep flight. Take the time to stop – and give yourself some credit for that.

3. Find healthy ways of dealing with your stress. I remember seeing a poster hanging somewhere years ago titled 'Top 10 Reasons Why I Procrastinate' and topping the list at number one was 'dot' – and that's all that is on the poster. The 'author' of the poster didn't get around to listing the other nine reasons! But seriously, procrastination is a massive trigger for stress in lots of people, particularly nowadays when work follows so many of us home through a phone or a tablet.

I recall being at a pre-Kilimanjaro trip meeting, where all of us agreed to take on four tasks. Twenty minutes after that meeting, the person chairing that night's meeting rang me to talk about my four tasks, and I replied: 'They're done. I couldn't have any of them hanging over me for days and weeks on end.' The 'Just Do It' mantra has become something I've lived by during my sobriety. It's symptomatic of my addictive personality. I'm all in. That's always been part of my composition. But channelling that to something other than my next brandy and milk is altogether more satisfying. It's been life-affirming.

There was this one person I used to work with and more than a few conversations she generated while sharing a lift went something like this:

> 'My boyfriend doesn't love me. I can't pay my mortgage; the exhaust pipe is hanging off the car.'

I kid you not, a further dozen negatives followed that triple crown of woe. So, you'd be talking about 15 different negatives, 15 different stressors experienced while sharing a lift, and it's not as if we were heading to the top of the Empire State Building either. We'd reach our floor, the doors open, she pops out with a smile on her face while I'm left there like I'd just spent three minutes attempting to dodge a right hand from Anthony Joshua.

One particular morning, I made a choice. As I staggered out of the lift, I chucked the key for the lift into the first available bin. If you surround yourself with positive people, you will develop greater levels of positivity. Now you won't turn into Mary Poppins, and you may never desire to be a life coach like Tony Robbins, but life gets that bit groovier when we've got more good vibes to tap into. We cannot be surprised that if we surround ourselves with hostile, negative, glass-half-empty types, that some of that shady mojo is going to ingrain itself into us over time.

Now of course there are times when we cannot avoid difficult people but we can choose how we deal with their negativity, how it impacts on us and how we interact with others. We really shouldn't keep our enemies closer to us than our friends. We're not all running Mafia empires after all. Again, to intone Mr Bueller, stop and look around. And specifically look at the people around you and take note of their dominant personality traits. We can't all be swans and find a mate for perpetuity. But we can choose our company. We can choose who influences us positively, just as you or I can in return when it comes to our own personal and professional circles. Do what Indiana Jones did when pursuing the Holy Grail. Choose wisely.

Learning how to manage your time can also play its part and this leads me to a conversation I had with a guy who had a bad back. He told me how bad the pain was, the amount of physiotherapy he was receiving, the medication he was on for it and so on – everything he told me about his back was a negative. The idea that the physio he was receiving was actually helping him in the long term appeared to be largely lost on him. There appeared to be no light getting in. Anyway, I wondered could he spare 10 minutes each day to stretch, which he responded to positively. To which I replied:

'Well if you were to stretch for ten minutes a day, seven days a week, four weeks a month, twelve months a year and if we agreed to meet one year from now, you'll have done fifty-six hours of flexibility work and I can guarantee that you won't have a pain in your back, and doing that exercise for just ten minutes a day won't have taken a single note out of your pocket.'

In an era where far too many of us find ourselves lamenting the lack of a spare minute, it's important that we use some of those spare minutes we do have, away from the cut and thrust of personal and/or professional life, and recognise that there are destinies we can control. And for me, it all comes down to what we prioritise: we have to prioritise the actions which lead to the solution of any problem. Otherwise, the problem will take out a long-term lease, seeping into every facet of your life and do untold damage not only to you but to those you interact with. Taking the time for the self also represents an investment in those you care most about.

How we manage our time must rank chiefly on our daily to-do list – and, yes, I have such a list of my own, an ever-present paper on my desk at De La Salle and it's the last thing I tend to at work every evening. So, with the following day in mind, I write down tomorrow's date and what I have to do on that list and when I return to work the following morning, it's there for me. I've inked it down in my workplace, therefore I don't need to bring it home with me. Simple? Yes. Beneficial? Enormously.

I'm an advocate of the SAS maxim: Preparation prevents piss-poor performance. If you prepare and plan, you can reduce stress and make life that little easier. Consider this: there are 24 hours in each and every day – 60 minutes in an hour, 60 seconds in a minute, all of which comes to 86,400 seconds daily. It's a finite amount of time, but I'd wager that a lot of us still have as many as ten tasks to do heading into the final quarter of that day. That's pressure we don't need. And we can avoid it.

Of course I experience stress on a regular basis, but I've found my own way of countering its worst excesses. I heard a dietitian speaking at a conference and she put it simply and bluntly: if you feel crap, you're going to eat crap and vice versa. When we're stressed, there's always the temptation to make the trip to the chipper or take a tub of ice cream out of the freezer. While there'll be the five-plus minutes of a sugar- or beef-dripping-inspired high, an hour later or the following morning, there will be that sickly feeling and the realisation that you're putting on weight, and then the extended downer that invariably follows. The day you tell yourself your arse does indeed 'look big in this' ought to be the day you hit the handbrake and declare 'enough'. You wouldn't pour a soft drink into your car engine as it would damage the mechanics, and the fact that we men in particular pay more attention to the care of our cars than the condition of ourselves is an itch we ought to scratch into the past tense.

I am a recent convert to yoga. And at the end of my first class, we went into what's known as the 'Corpse Pose', more commonly known as Shavasana, a period of guided meditation. To my surprise, I found myself breathing deeper and deeper. I was relishing the moment when all of a sudden, the peace was broken by a whole-snorted snore. Now I felt a bit put out – I'd paid my tenner for the class and felt like I was receiving an immediate benefit – and one of the class had gone full Rip Van Winkle on us. But then I realised I was the sound merchant in chief – I'd fallen asleep in the middle of the class! I was so deeply relaxed; it was as if I was a third party to the unwelcome interruption.

With that in mind, albeit ideally without the snoring, doing something new can positively impact on the stress levels in your life. And for me, one of the major problems a lot of people whom I deal with share with me can be quite specific to sleep. Too many of us, I feel, categorise sleep as being the end of today, whereas I feel we'd all be better served if we considered it as the start of tomorrow. If you've ever had an unresolved argument late in the day, those tough words will still be whirring around in a negative spin cycle at the very time you need to clear your head, quieten your mind and prepare to rest. And if you've not restored your body chemistry that night, that will serve to negatively impact upon the following day, how you feel and how you interact with others. Bear in mind the words of Roman philosopher Seneca, who said:

> 'The rational soul is stronger than any kind of fortune – from its own share it guides its affairs here or there, and is itself the cause of a happy or miserable life.'

Sleep is a stress cleanser. It's the best wash we can give ourselves each and every day. And it can help us remember that we remain masters of our destiny.

While us older fogeys cut out the double espressos after 3 p.m. or may choose to eat within 12-hour windows – 7 a.m. to 7 p.m. has become a popular option on that front – the reality for young adults and teenagers is somewhat different in this increasingly online world which they predominantly populate.

Social media accounts project idealised versions of what life is like: much of its significance revolves around how many friends you have, how perfect your hair and make-up are or how ripped your body is. After all, there are not too many posts about having a bunged-up sinus or experiencing diarrhoea during an ascent of Kilimanjaro. We can read those illusory *'la vita e bella'* posts late at night, as the soggy biscuit drops into the mug, and be left feeling like our own lives are low-key and almost devoid of worth in comparison. Most of us can move on from that thought. But others, often young and impressionable, may not move on so rapidly. And that can lead to devastating outcomes.

Fr Paschal Moore, a parish priest in south Kilkenny, addressing a congregation in the wake of 14-year-old Elisha Gault's tragic death in March 2018, knew he would have to choose his words with surgical precision at her funeral.

For a man who had previously officiated at 25 ceremonies where the life of the deceased was later adjudicated by coroners as death by suicide, Fr Moore was cognisant he had to share a direct message with the devastated teenagers sat in row after row in front of him that morning. And this is what he said:

> 'We all have our worries, our stresses and our anxieties, and stress can be hopeless. The problem arises when our anxiety takes over every moment of our lives...we all need support, every one of us needs support from the oldest to the youngest of us. We need people who will listen, people who will talk to us, people who will be a shoulder to lean on. Today, boys and girls, I would encourage you to form a support network around yourselves...I would encourage you also to turn off your iPhone every now and again. Facebook

is wonderful at times and people boast about how many friends they have on Facebook, but your friends on Facebook are artificial friends. What you need are real people around you: real, genuine, caring people and I would encourage you, every one of you, to find a real, good support network for yourselves.'[16]

The mind is easily drawn to the negative, to the 'poor me' sentiment. That can become a cycle from which the only outcome some feel is left available to them is the one we all know there's no returning from. Ten people die by suicide in Ireland each week. It's why 'Share the Load' is more than just a catchy phrase on a car sticker. It's why I'm so passionate about the Pieta House message. It's why I've walked from one end of Ireland to the other with a washing machine on my back, and took on Kilimanjaro with the same contraption.

Yes, life can present us with challenges, but we can surmount most of them. We can make subtle and positive changes to our lives, and finding ways of reducing stress can play a huge role in that, because if you don't control your life, your life will control you. We remain masters of our destinies, and that thought is worth retaining, cherishing even, particularly just before the dawn.

16

Life Under Lockdown

'Don't behave as if you are destined to live forever. What's fated hangs over you. As long as you live and while you can, become good now.'

Marcus Aurelius, *Meditations*, 4.17

Like a sizeable portion of the Irish adult population, the Covid-19 pandemic got me into the garden, fixing, moving and removing stuff gathered over more years than most of us readily admit to. A great many people decided that the global health emergency was as good a time as any to order a new shed, but to make space for our new arrival we had to decommission everything that the old shed was housing. There, I found sections of old trampoline that wouldn't fit into the bin, about a dozen broken swingball sets, an assortment of frisbees, flat footballs that I couldn't find the valve for, etc. And it didn't end there.

Fionn and I were making steady progress through the detritus – well, at least that's what I thought – but Maeve felt the work required a gear change so she laid into the task with her customary gusto. 'God, there's some rubbish out here,' she said to me, 'and just look at all the bottles, they must have been in here for years.' Those words hit me like bombs dropping from a payload and I instantly flashed back to the last time I laid eyes on those bottles. There was Calvet and definitely a couple of Sangre de Toros too – I used to like the little plastic bull that hung off that particular bottle – and there were some other emptied bottles of Merlot out there as well. Gazing at them had the finger-clicking-like effect of sending me back in time to many a 'school night' when I frequented that shed, then stocked with full wine bottles. Back then, for me, opening a bottle was like turning on a tap and just letting it flow. I simply couldn't drink enough. So most nights of the week, alone in that shed, on the pretence that I was nipping out to get a bottle for us to share, I drained another one before I returned indoors. It literally was a case of 'Glug, glug, glug, glug – gone.' That was 15 years ago.

I didn't retreat to the shed to drown my sorrows on account of a big flare-up with Maeve or due to some awful childhood experience that had just flashed upon the inward eye. While my mental health wasn't what it ought to have been at the time, I drank the way I did out of habit and because I could afford it. Many of those bottles had been transported – nursed home even – in the back of our car after holidays in France. A joke I regularly used to crack was that if we ever crashed outside Rosslare, given all the wine we brought back with us, the kids would drown in the back of the car! This was when a bottle of wine in France was selling for a tenth or less of the price for the same brand sold in Ireland, and that shed was brimming with wine – you're talking in the region of 140 bottles. Such was my pride in so vast a collection that I laid them all out in our sitting room for a photo akin to Hemingway in Africa posing with a slain animal whose head would end up on his sitting room wall. That was my trophy collection. But there was no logic to it. No reason. It was pure addiction.

The key to addiction is dishonesty. But if you unlock the dishonesty, you'll go a long way towards breaking the addiction. My intelligence, by and large, allowed me to hide my alcoholism convincingly for quite some time both at home and at work. Having knocked back a bottle, I'd walk back into the sitting room and have a glass of wine with Maeve. She'd then ask me if I'd like another glass. 'Ah, no,' I remember saying more than once to her. 'Just the one will do me tonight.' Minutes beforehand, I'd necked down a full bottle. That was the norm. That was all the time.

I stood in a shed, in the dark, night after night, slugging wine. How did I reach that point in my life? Even now, being sober and as far removed from my active alcoholism as I reckon I'll ever be, I still wonder how I broke that cycle. What provoked me into honesty to such a degree that in the midst of Covid-19's first wave I found myself hosting 1,000 people on a stress management webinar for AIB? I've certainly got a good grounding when it comes to living through difficult times and extricating myself from a chaotic lifestyle, but I still have times when I can scarcely believe people would turn to me for advice on how to manage anxiety.

The guy in the garden shed 15 years ago, the fella in thrall to liquor, convincing himself there'd be no negative consequence to curating a wine-soaked bubble, would have been incredulous about such a prospect. But here I am. I've unlocked the dishonesty and in so doing improved my life beyond all measure. Living is a significant step up on existing. It's a train I'm in no rush to depart from.

As part of the measures implemented to mitigate the spread of Covid-19, Irish schools were closed on Thursday, 12 March 2020, turning life as we knew it on its head. Via the school intercom, we were informed that all students were to go home and take their books with them – they could be at home for a while. Soon afterwards, the teachers assembled in the staffroom and the principal announced that we were closing. The concept of social or physical distancing did not factor into our thinking at that moment in time. We sat in the same places we'd always sat in close proximity to each other – some of us have done that for decades. It was the last such time we spent together as a staff in the 2019/20 school year – the year of no standardised Leaving and Junior Certificate examinations.

As I left De La Salle, I rang Maeve. She panicked instantly, querying: 'Oh my God, what will we eat? I'll go to the supermarket on the way home.' She was far from alone in contemplating this course of action as natural human panic kicked in across the country, prompting an unprecedented rush in toilet roll sales. 'Don't go to the shop,' I replied. 'I already have lots of stuff bought.' During the previous few weeks, as the initial emergency in Wuhan became a devastating killer in the Italian city of Bergamo, I'd been buying some additional groceries. I don't do anxiety or panic anymore so my way of dealing with what was coming down the tracks was to be organised. Real Baden-Powell stuff.

Now when our kids found my stash, they were disgusted: you're talking brown rice, organic quinoa, wholegrain pasta and the like. It was low-fat, no-sugar goodness all the way. I told Maeve: 'Come home and we'll be together. Everything is in hand and everything is fine.' And she did just that. I genuinely thought everything would be fine inside our own four walls, but over the first four days of the lockdown I lost sight of what has made me stronger, healthier and happier. I found myself watching a variety of TV news channels from one end of the day to the next, over-dosing on catastrophe. The apocalypse proved initially inescapable for me. As someone who cannot watch horror movies, primarily due to how powerful my imagination is and given my tendency to visualise, digesting so much appalling news weighed heavily on me. I was overloading my psyche with a frenzied level of panic and worry. I actually freaked out and had panic attacks for the first time in over a decade.

On the second morning at home, prior to having my breakfast like I do every single morning, I poured myself a glass of water only for my swallow reflex to go AWOL on me. It got to the point where I couldn't swallow. 'Oh crap,' I said to myself. 'Not this. Not now.' It was a horrible callback to that phase in my life when I'd just stopped drinking, when I didn't feel any sense of calm and control about what lay ahead of me. That night in bed, I had nightmares and night sweats; I had to change my t-shirt such were my perspiration levels. I was overthinking everything. By day three, my heart was racing and I was worrying about my next panic attack. A panic attack might be a relatively infrequent occurrence but the worry about having one is a different level of anxiety: where might I be if it happens? Will I make a show of myself if I have another one? It's akin to pouring petrol on a fire you never set out to light in the first place. I was worrying about worrying.

It got to the stage where I literally had to sit down and grab a pen and paper. I began to write about how I was feeling, why I was feeling like this and what I needed to do to get back to where I've largely been throughout my sobriety. Anxiety, pressure and stress had thundered across my mindset like a rapidly advancing infantry. These were facets of my being I'd largely tempered for over a decade. I don't pretend they're not there, after all we need a certain level of stress in our lives, but not to the point where it prevents you from functioning at home or in work. So I started re-writing the list I'd worked on during those first few weeks and months of getting sober and the more I wrote, the more the pressure levels diminished. The wave of terror began to abate. Things grew calmer for me. As I know how powerful and debilitating anxiety can be, and because I spend every day of my life focused on not allowing my body to produce those debilitating chemicals because I simply don't want to feel that way, that 'fire' was extinguished. Peace had been restored to the Republic of Enda.

I have to stay true to myself and I do that by re-enforcing my strengths while remaining cognisant of my demerits. But I cannot allow myself to be ruled by negativity. That's not who I am now. I can't be that guy anymore. In a bid to positively counter that imp on my shoulder, I sought out a fresh challenge and it didn't take too long to find one. I cracked open the laptop and researched a course on digital marketing, an area I knew very little about despite my public speaking career. Occupying my brain through learning new skills and remaining open to new ideas was both a practical step and a coping mechanism. Over the course of the first few lectures, I realised how digitally disorganised I was. Each lecture generated ten tasks and after three weeks I had at least three months' work to do, and this allowed me to refocus. And boy, was I glad of that.

During the Belfast to Waterford walk, I was blessed to have a team of people who, in rotation, walked alongside me for considerable distances each day. They'd ask me things like 'what did you think of that house over there' or 'do you remember that lovely woman who came along with us for a few miles yesterday morning?' In the there and then, while I was walking, I'd have no memory whatsoever of some faces and places. I've learned to concentrate so deeply that I could condense seven hours down to a minute or less, which was obviously a huge help given the physical turmoil the walk exposed me to. And that feeling rekindled as the lockdown restrictions began to ease to the point where we could invite a neighbour or friend into our garden for a coffee, having had no one outside of the family for company at home for almost three months. When we bade farewell to our first post-lockdown visitor I said to Maeve: 'It feels like I've only been home for two days.' Compressing time like that has proven enormously beneficial for me. That I had been learning new skills and attempting to improve myself both mentally and physically throughout the late spring/early summer has made life more tolerable for me; it's also added value to it.

Every single day throughout the duration of 'Phase One' (12 March to 18 May) of the Government's pandemic regulations, I called three different people. At no stage on any of those calls did I apologise for not ringing sooner or anything like that, nor was it a case of me not calling someone because it was their turn to call me. The only one who loses out in that scenario, playing by those made-up rules, is me. Family, friends, colleagues, people who travelled with me to Africa: I rang them all and we had some wonderful conversations. Sometimes I went into autopilot and told the same story to 20 people – but I never, ever got the same story back. A little bit of news or gossip was like a gold nugget during the height of the lockdown, so I took whatever news came my way during such calls and, like a squirrel gathering nuts for his family, I doled out the details to the others. Starved for wider company and hungry for information, 'a man's gotta do what a man's gotta do'.

After the initial wobble, I was still out of bed every morning at 5:30 a.m. I wasn't willing to let that waver. I maintained good eating habits, got in some yoga, walked miles every day – all of which kept my edginess and anxiety in check. I felt a sense of guilt due to the fact that I was enjoying the lockdown while tens of thousands were dying or lying gravely ill in pandemic hotspots in Italy, Spain, the UK, Iran and the United States. But this was not a time of personal misery for me. I had my family around me, enjoying the best possible Groundhog Day. We sat together, we ate together, we told stories and we laughed. The kids had no one but each other for two solid months and I think they learned to like each other as young adults in a manner that the pace of regular life, given their own friends and their own hobbies, simply doesn't permit. At one stage I heard Maeve, in the same tone of voice one adopts when talking about a puppy, asking them both: 'Will one of you take him [as in me] out later?' Sure you could only laugh!

The importance of being sociable was made plain to me during Covid-19. If we talk to each other more, spend more time with each other and encourage, question and challenge each other, we'll enhance our own lives and the lives of those we care about. Surely that's what we're here for, as opposed to spending 72 hours in the car as I did in the month prior to lockdown. During the first month of Covid, I drove for a grand total of one hour. I'm not going back to that extent of driving ever again. Eating a chicken sandwich from a carton while sat in a motorway rest area is something I'll be doing a lot less of from now on. The lockdown called our bluff. We have the time to do the things that matter if we prioritise what truly counts. A lot of us took the time to literally get our houses – and sheds – in order. And it shouldn't stop there.

Giving ourselves the time to test what Abraham Maslow champions in his hierarchy of needs in terms of (from the base up) physiological needs, safety needs, love and belonging, esteem, and self-actualisation is clearly a journey worth taking. We all possess the capacity for re-invention. We all have the power to be better versions of ourselves. Sadly, most people don't go down that route due to being held back by fear. What did I do? I stopped drinking. I carried a washing machine on my back from Belfast to Waterford and then most of the way up Kilimanjaro. And now I've written a book about all of this. We shouldn't be so fearful of hitting the reset button and we should never allow ourselves to be imprisoned by fear. There's simply too much living to do.

17

Undiscovered Countries and Magic Moments

It's no surprise that I get asked about the next challenge quite a lot. Will I round out my washing machine adventures with a satisfying, sinew-straining, trilogy-sealing finale? Or will I finally decommission the Beko, get a bit of sense and look after my body in a slightly more tolerable manner? Well, my most immediate plan is to stay married because to commit to nine months of 14-hour training weeks, in addition to all the media, charity and physiotherapy commitments, would take its toll on the whole household. There's more than just me who needs considering. We've raised over €280,000 so far, and that's enormously satisfying. Lives will be saved thanks to that money and knowing that fills me with a great sense of wellbeing, more than compensating for my not reaching the summit of Kilimanjaro. So, to be honest, I'm not racing for something new. Well, at least not too intently.

But inevitably there's a 'but'. There has to be. Once you've looked over a few different hills to see what's on the other side, you do so cognisant that there's plenty more to peer over. Getting up on the scales after spells of undisciplined eating isn't good for the jowl or midriff – it's even worse for the ego – and I know that when I'm focused in my training, seeing colours amidst my sweat-caked state pleases me. I've got no off switch. When I'm in the gym, working out in the absence of a defined goal, the little voice in the back of my head is constantly querying how much more I'd get out of the engine if I had a challenge pencilled in a few months down the line. When I was preparing for Kilimanjaro, I was training twice a day, wearing an oxygen deprivation mask and putting myself through hell to reach peak aerobic condition, and it's certainly helpful to have a definite goal in mind. That little voice is never too far away once I'm in gym mode. It's certainly made a case to me when it comes to the next challenge and while there's nothing set in stone, I can't help thinking there's another adventure out there.

The North Pole Marathon retains some appeal, but the organisers aren't too keen on a man who has just bade farewell to his 40s carrying a large metal box in the slaughtering cold for at least half a day. Everything about the event is savage, which probably explains why I'm so drawn to it. I've seen footage of Russian paratroopers jumping from an aircraft, with a slew of cargo boxes already parachuted beneath them, from which they'll set up the landing strip and tents for the marathon competitors. It's gloriously masochistic, with entrants taking between 10 and 11 hours to complete the distance given the conditions. Now, the €14,000 entry fee is a sizeable consideration in its own right but if a corporate type was willing to cover that, and if I could raise up to, say, €70,000, I think I could justify taking it on. I'd probably have to use a facsimile of a washing machine, as a regular metal model would be out of bounds given the conditions. Perhaps I'd carry its equivalent weight; there'd certainly be an appeal to such an icy challenge. But it'd probably be an individual experience; I know that would make it fundamentally different to Belfast to Waterford and Kilimanjaro. Not having my family involved would be a major disincentive, but I've learned in life to 'never say never'. It's vital to leave your imagination unfiltered and open to any potential eventuality.

The Great Wall of China would be an extraordinary albeit difficult undertaking. Since coming back from Tanzania, I've envisaged jetting off with 30 Irish people to cover seven or eight marathon lengths on the Great Wall, which hasn't a flat section of any kind along its astounding length (the Ming Great Wall alone is 5,500 miles long), weaving through 15 different provinces. A marathon for me, with washing machine in tow, would be six hours on a relatively benign surface. On the Great Wall, I'd be constantly going up and down tens of thousands of steps and I'd have to wonder how my knees and ankles would cope with that over eight days. In the months after Kilimanjaro, I was badly beaten up. I had pains and aches that I'd never previously experienced but I know if you don't fill your life with a dream, you're just surviving. And I don't want to just survive. I want every mile on the clock to count for something. That's what keeps the engine fuelled and almost certainly means there's another challenge ahead of me.

Why? Well, it fills my life. It's not that my life is particularly empty – I've a wonderful family and great friends in addition to teaching and public speaking – but if you don't have something different and fantastical to look forward to, if you don't have that next memory filler, what else is there? Why settle for survival when you can live and maybe help out a few lost souls along the way? I relish the big picture: wider canvases need more colour and creativity before they can be exhibited. And when I approach the beginning of the end, hopefully several decades from now, I want to linger in a grand hall, even if it's just in my mind's eye, and spend a pleasant hour or two scanning the canvas of my life. I want it to be packed with detail: faces, places, colours, the whole nine yards. My own masterpiece. I want that deep satisfactory exhalation. 'To think I did all that,' as Old Blue Eyes crooned it. That's what I want. But I won't reach that destination by settling for survival. That's why I won't take the easy train between now and the ultimate endgame. That's not who I am. That's why every day should be attacked and celebrated in equal measure.

There's a myriad of other challenges I'd like to take on but there are family and professional considerations that would need weighing up before leaping down another rabbit hole. I'd love to complete 52 marathons over 52 weekends, carrying the washing machine through 52 different towns across the country, distributing hundreds of flyers with self-help and donation numbers, encouraging people to 'Share the Load'. That would mean six to seven hours of walking with a washing machine every weekend for a year, ultimately clocking in 2,163 kilometres (Dublin to Barcelona, plus change). If your goal isn't scary, then it's not good enough: taking on this challenge would scare the life out of me. A marathon, without a washing machine, is a huge physical undertaking. The thought of doing one every week for an entire year, covering the distance of Kilimanjaro 367 times in total, with the Beko is scarifying – but nonetheless appealing.

A fundraising offshoot of such a challenge could, for example, lead to the creation of a memorial to all people in Ireland who have lost their lives through suicide. Not to highlight the manner in which they died, but moreso to establish it as a memorial of hope, to show to people, even in their darkest hour, that there is always an alternative. We've lived in a society where, for decades, people who died by suicide were buried in unconsecrated ground. The same society which brushed child abuse under the carpet, a society which buried babies in unmarked graves because they were born out of wedlock, a society which debased and criminalised people who were attracted to others of the same sex.

The irony that many of those responsible for leading societal thinking on these fronts could not live up to their own words is not lost on the generations damaged by their actions. Many of whom, sadly, couldn't escape such darkness and saw suicide as their only remedy. A memorial of hope in a modern Ireland still grappling with the appalling legacies of institutional, clerical and domestic abuse would, I feel, show that we now treat and value people differently and that we aspire to judge them on how they treat us, through the actions they take in their lives, and how we in turn support them. I'd love to make that happen, to be involved in physically manifesting a symbol which shows that there is a better way, that we care, that, as John Lennon once said, love is the answer. And we know that, for sure. The huge rockface above Waterford Railway Station, ironically known as 'Mount Misery', would be a fantastic spot for such a memorial. Literally transposing hope onto misery has a good ring to it. Rio has Christ the Redeemer. London has Big Ben. Imagine if Waterford had the Statue of Hope? Now there's a thought.

When I finished the Ironman, I wondered what could possibly top that, but I soon learned as I committed to other challenges that you always top what you've previously achieved. The only limits you set are forged between your own ears. When I finished the Belfast Marathon, I thought I'd never be as fit as that again. Five years later, I was six times fitter. Two years on from that, I'd doubled my fitness levels again. And two years later, I was walking from Belfast to Waterford with a washing machine on my back. The perpetual ability to dream isn't lost on me, and I must confess to having a bizarre imagination. My head is on fire, 24/7. So, on the whole, I want to commit to another adventure, but that Eureka moment has to hit me right between the eyes, just like when you meet the right person or you hear the right song at a wedding and you just know you've got to dance. I want to do something and pursue it with everything I have, but it has to be the right thing. It has to be. However, it will not be something at altitude. Being as sick as I was in Tanzania is a total turn-off to any more elevated adventuring.

***

'Are you awake?' Maeve questioned one morning while on holidays in the Canaries. It just so happened I was - and wide-eyed at that.

'Do you want to do something different?' she then asked, and what with me being a man and all, my mind started to race.

'Oh boy,' I said to myself. 'It's Christmas!'

I replied to Maeve: 'Yeah. Absolutely. What do you have in mind?'

Maeve said: 'You know, I've never seen a sunrise. Do you want to go down to the beach with me and watch the sunrise?'

The bed was warm, the linen was pristine and my mind had gone where many male minds tend to go when a suggestion is made beneath the sheets, but I soon switched tack and up we got. It was just gone 5 a.m., and the African air was warm and inviting as we approached a beachside rock in total darkness. We sat on that rock and the sun came up. Jesus, what an experience! It's a moment I've treasured ever since, a moment I tap into during those days and nights which prove a touch more difficult to negotiate. As much as I love looking forward to what's next, that particularly memory is as golden as the first rays we watched together that morning, upon an island still in slumber.

**

There's a 2006 team photograph in the assembly hall of De La Salle College, and Enda 1.0 is stood there in the corner of the snap. The Cheltenham National Hunt Horse Racing Festival was on that same week and I spent the three days after that big colleges' match in the pub. Today, I don't recognise the guy standing there. He's not the man I've seen in the mirror every morning over the past 11 alcohol-free years. He had no big plan. His only plans were the next pint, the next session, the next excuse to go drinking, to go to a soccer match which he'd no interest in but did so knowing it was totally legitimate to turn up full of beer and then drink more after the full-time whistle. He told everyone that he was having a great time. He wasn't. He was miserable. He was limping through life, slinging between all too regular bouts of drunkenness. He was surviving. There was no living going on. I was like a vase with a broken chip, but I was a decidedly Irish vase; the chances were that the rest of the vase would end up shattered.

Japanese culture is altogether different to ours in so many ways, and not just limited to stunning decorum and indisputable punctuality. They'd see a vase with a chipped area and fill in the crack with, say, gold or silver, and also keep the detached piece. So not only do they save the vase, but they add value to it; an object which has survived some form of physical damage. While my drunken years were downright shitty, utterly miserable and without a genuine sense of purpose, I do know, from this juncture in my life, that they still contained value and that what I didn't do then has helped to motivate me when it comes to everything I've done since. I don't settle for survival anymore. There's too much living to do. That's who I am now. Positively or negatively, action changes your life. Taking that positive action and running with it is where I'm at now, it's what I've done for over eleven years, and it's a fantastic place to be.

***

'Are you not fed up with charity work' is a question that gets put to me time and time again. I get way more from it than I give so the answer, each and every time to that question, is a huge and decisive no. The people I've met through the two big challenges and various other fundraisers have added meaning, purpose and energy to my life. Beating up my body has socially enriched me and helped to make me a better person. Three days into the Kilimanjaro trek, above the cloud line, Maeve and I unzipped the tent and gazed into the distance. And in that moment, I thought about the many decisions I had made and the people I had met which had led me onto that mountainside. Every single time I'm in doubt about myself and what's going on in my life, I go back to that morning, above the cloud line, sitting in absolute contentment alongside my wife.

Bloody hell. To think we did all that. But there's more to do. I just know there is.

Appendices

Lisa Walsh: Enda and Me

My family will tell all and sundry that I get a three- or four-year itch to take on something, an impulse which propels me off on some crazy adventure or mad challenge of some kind. Lo and behold, while I was on Facebook one Saturday during the autumn of 2016, this mad idea - the Pieta Challenge with Enda O'Doherty - popped up, and the itch returned. I mentioned it to my fiancé, Stephen, and he told me: 'You can't, Lisa. You just can't do it.'

He reminded me that in 2005 I'd broken my back - in two places - after slipping on the stairs at home. I was standing in my socks on a varnished staircase and I did a banana peel slip off the second step. My feet went clean from under me and I landed on the corner of a step on my back and went down five more steps. I'd never broken a bone before in my life, so this was some introduction to such a world of discomfort, my body deeply blackened with bruising from the back of my head to the back of my knees. I ended up in a steel body harness for nine months.

Apparently, I'd broken my back in the 'best possible way', damaging my T10 and T11 vertebrae. Had the injury been one vertebra lower, I would have nipped the spinal cord and would have probably been para-lysed. Talk about a game of inches. I ended up having ten people lifting me onto a wooden board, a brace on my neck, getting log-rolled, the whole lot. Following my liberation from the body harness, eighteen months of physiotherapy followed. It was an incredibly tough time, but I got through it and it put things into perspective for me. If I'm ten minutes late for something, so what? I feel I know what really matters now. I work with people with disabilities, some of whom have had major accidents and suffered acquired brain injuries. I realise how close I was to being in a similar position to the people I help. I knew how lucky I was, but I also knew I needed to get out and do something, to put my healed body to good use. And when you've gone from being handwashed by someone else for months and experiencing difficulty in putting on a sock on your own, to the joy of regaining full mobility, the determination to get out there is understandable. Life has to carry on and I wasn't going to let any challenge pass me by again.

But still, when I mentioned the idea at home, Stephen, quite logically, put it like this: 'You're just not going to be able to take on something like that, up a huge mountain, carrying a backpack for hours at a time. It's just going to be too much of a strain on you.' That my first thought on seeing Enda's Facebook page was that this was something I could do and would enjoy doing, probably tells you how mad I am in a sense and how determined I am in another. It probably explains why myself and Enda get on so well.

I had some history on the hiking front. Back when I was living in Kildare, in the late noughties, I'd decided to walk the Inca Trail as a fundraiser for a Peruvian orphanage – I'd only started going out with Stephen at the time – and on the Monday before I set off, he bought me roller-skates as a romantic gesture. So we went out for dinner, had a few cocktails and after all of that, I thought it'd be a good idea to try on my new skates and we headed out to a nearby hill, similar to Bunker's Hill in Waterford city (the closest thing we have to Patrick's Hill in Cork), and things, initially, went really well. But at the end of the hill, I was too straight and I came down on my knee very heavily. I was in bits.

Now I'd been training for a year to get ready for the Inca Trail and had raised a lot of money so I knew what I had to do. I went to the doctor and requested all the drugs which could be legally prescribed to me - he'd completed the trail himself and knew what I'd put into my training - so he did what he could do legally and sent me on my way. I said absolutely nothing about my tumble to the organisers. I travelled to Peru on my own, I completed the trail but when I got back, I discovered I needed exploratory surgery such was the damage to my knee. And Stephen felt he needed to remind me about that too. 'Not a hope,' he said. 'We're talking about the tallest free-standing mountain in the world here.' Now it's not as if Stephen was issuing a diktat to me - he was naturally worried about me taking on something as colossal as Kilimanjaro given my history. But just like me and my busted knee prior to Peru, I knew what I wanted to do. I loved the idea of taking on the mountain with a bunch of Irish people and to raise some money while doing it. It all made sense to me.

Within four days of Enda's Facebook page for Kilimanjaro going live, I told my family I was thinking of committing to the challenge and they collectively went: 'Oh Jesus Christ.' I had to have it pointed it out to me that whenever I said 'I'm thinking' about doing something, it meant I'd made up my mind and that I was just running it by them to see how mad they thought it was - cue laughter all round! But the consensus immediately emerged: it was a mad idea but there was no point in attempting to talk me out of doing it. So the following day, I rang Enda and he gave me his 40-minute speech that he would ultimately give to everyone who made the trip, about what this challenge meant, how brilliant an idea it was and what it would mean for people back home going through a crisis. By the time Enda had stopped talking - now he was out on a training walk at the time with the washing machine on his back, panting and ranting - I had to point out to him that I'd made my mind up prior to the phone call and that I'd only contacted him to tell him I was signing up. But it was hard to get a word in edgeways: remember, this is Enda we're talking about! And with the world being so small and all, it turned out that my dad had fitted a kitchen for Enda two weeks before I called him. Talk about *Sliding Doors* stuff - well, fitted kitchens but you know what I mean.

To be honest, I'd a totally different impression of Enda when I compared his Facebook page to the man I ended up speaking to. The page struck such an official, straight-laced tone, and then when I spoke to him all I could think was that he was just an ordinary Waterford lad; granted a long-term blow-in but a Waterford lad nonetheless. I'd no personal connection to Enda at all, and even when I first looked at the Facebook page, it never struck me that this challenge was being coordinated by a man living just out the road from me. I didn't know all that much about the Belfast to Waterford walk either but once I met him, I liked him from the get-go and we soon established that we had lots of mutual connections, that being the way of the Irish and all.

I'd only just been added to a WhatsApp group for the trek - there was about 12 of us signed up at that stage - and I was sitting in my office at St Brigid's Family and Community Centre on Waterford's Lower Yellow Road one day and my phone was pinging. As I walked down to reception, there was a man from work I didn't know too well looking at me quite intently; at first I didn't really know what to make of it. But as I walked out of the kitchen he said to me: 'Lisa, I'm Daire Grant and I believe you're coming to Kilimanjaro with me.' It turned out that Daire had been working in an office across from me for one day a week over the previous two years at that stage and we'd never met each other until the day after I signed up for the challenge. That made me think that this was meant to be. I knew what I wanted to do and I was committed to it. So I trained hard, I fundraised diligently, met my targets on both fronts as best I could and boarded that plane to Addis Ababa, with Enda, the disassembled washing machine and the rest of the group.

Now I was one of the luckier ones out there as the altitude wasn't a source of much discomfort for me. An hour into the first day, the combination of altitude and dust had knocked the stuffing out of one of my training partners, Julie, who I'd met up with most Sundays to scale the hills around Glendalough (a minimum trek of four to five hours), which she bounded up like a gazelle. Julie has asthma too and she was almost immediately knocked for six. She didn't look a likely finisher from an early stage, but it says something about Julie that it took until summit night for her to be told that her race was run. Not too many of us had zeroed in on the hour-to-hour specifics, let alone the day-to-day elements of what Kilimanjaro would take out of us; if we had, we probably would have thought twice. And then of course there was that poor girl from Cork, Majella Duffy, who lost her life on the mountain, by which time all of us were safely back home. And that awful news made a lot of us realise just how big a deal taking on Kilimanjaro was. Life and death stuff. And you never know when it's going to come to your own door. You just never know.

Three weeks before we boarded the plane to Ethiopia, my sister, who has experienced a lot of mental health difficulties, attempted to take her life by suicide. An overdose. While I'd put in all the training, held several different fundraisers and so on in the months leading up to the trip, with the phrase 'it's okay not to be okay' running on repeat in my mind, that experience, the reality that we as a family had in facing this and coming to terms with it, doubled my determination to reach the summit. I've no doubt it got me up the mountain.

When we were in camp prior to taking on the Barranco Wall, I managed to reach my sister on the phone and I greeted her with 'How are you?' Those three words take on a lot more weight when someone you love has attempted to take their life. I never thought the Pieta House service was something I'd ever come into contact with, but three weeks before I left, that was my reality, accessing Pieta for my sister. She told me she was okay. I knew she wasn't. She wanted me to climb the mountain and she hoped I'd see the task out. By the time our chat ended, I was in hysterics and everyone in the mess tent was wondering what the hell was going on. Enda knew – I think one other person there knew at the time. I'd spoken to Enda to try to access services, and he did his best to look after me given how fragile I was at that moment. He's brilliant that way. But I decided to tell everyone in the tent what had happened three weeks previously and it was a relief to say it out loud. To 'Share the Load'. Even when I was at my lowest when it came to my back, being housebound and unable to wash myself, I'd never experienced a total sense of hope-lessness. That's not to say I didn't feel blue from time to time, but I could still only imagine how someone considering ending it all must feel. And that's why any back issues I might have had going up the mountain felt so small and immaterial. I just got on with it. I had to.

On summit night, after an hour-and-a-half's sleep and 40 minutes of layering up for the final upward push, we were split into two groups. I'd come a long way from not being able to manage the steps of Glen-dalough that first day's hiking, and while I wasn't at my physical best by then – few if any of us were – I was doubly determined to see this thing out. By the time the sun was coming up, we had reached Mawenzi Peak (5,149 metres/16,893 feet), one of two peaks on the summit of the mountain, but Uhuru Peak (5,895m/19,341 feet) lay that little bit beyond us – yet it was still an hour and a half away. We were so tired and by then I genuinely felt that my bolt was shot. I was positioned between two of our group, Aisling in front and Peter behind me, and they were doing all they could to keep me moving slowly forward. 'We're going to count to five and then we're going to take another step,' Peter said, over and over, as we literally edged towards the summit, with our breathing completely laboured by that point. One, two, three, four, five, and repeat: it sounds utterly basic but it worked. Peter threw his arms around my waist at one stage and said: 'We'll do ten this time,' and we did. And that kept me going. As we inched towards the summit, we saw another group, American I think, approaching the summit and I really thought I was hallucinating: one of them was in a full Batman costume. None of us said anything at the time and it was about 48 hours later before any of us brought up the Batman sighting, which thankfully hadn't been my imagination at work! By then we could laugh. We could breathe a little easier. We'd summited Kilimanjaro. Washing machine and all.

I only appreciated what Enda had persuaded and cajoled us all to do by the time I got home. This was actually a pretty big deal, and it became an even bigger deal when the news about Majella Duffy broke.

Climbing Kilimanjaro was a life-changer. I've made friends for life because of it – 'the Kili crew' as my non-mountain-trekking circle like to refer to them as – and a lot of them joined me on my hen night. We made so many wonderful connections during the trip and one man is responsible for that. And if Enda O'Doherty ever takes to Facebook again to lay down another challenge, I'll be on for another mad adventure – once I run it by Stephen of course!

Tim O'Carroll: Enda and Me

I first got to know Enda O'Doherty thanks to Leaving Certificate Geography grinds back in 2002/2003 while I was studying at Newtown School in Waterford city, literally up the road from Enda's day job at De La Salle. And from the get-go I thought there was something different about him – a teacher speaking on the same level as a humble student was positively unusual in my experience. He was incredibly chatty, quite bubbly and very easy to relate to. First and foremost, Enda told me what I needed to know to get over the line in the exam. He had a really straight way of framing the whole exam process in terms of pointing out what I needed to know and I found that very helpful, at a time in my life when there were a lot of academic balls to juggle.

While I bumped into Enda once or twice in Waterford beyond the Leaving, we didn't keep in touch in any sort of significant way. Time passed and some years later while I was working in Dublin for the fundraising website MyCharity.ie its marketing team issued a circular: they were seeking out people who had inspirational stories to share on a section of the website. By then Enda had a page on the site, so I connected with him via Facebook to ask if someone in our office could give him a shout and to share his Belfast to Waterford experience on a special section on our site. He was all on for that. So I put him in touch with one of my colleagues who interviewed him about the walk, which in turn led to a piece being published online. Just like the Leaving Cert had gone for me, the interview went well for Enda.

Several months later, when I caught wind of Enda's proposed Kilimanjaro challenge, I contacted him to offer my assistance to anyone who might be interested in online fundraising, which he was quite receptive to. But he speedily planted a seed in my own head about Kilimanjaro:

would I join him on the trip? He cheerily told me: 'Now all you have to do is raise four grand!' Now this was a pretty big outlay, but having thought about it on 'once in a lifetime' grounds, but largely due to Enda's powers of persuasion, I decided to give it a go. Personally, this was new fundraising territory for me and it did feel a little daunting. But much to my delight, the initial thought devoted to the task outweighed the actual task of raising the money, and that came as a real surprise to me. It turns out that you'd raise €4,000 pretty quickly if the cause demanded it. I arranged a few events, including a 100-kilometre cycle for Pieta House in September 2016, which raised €800. My mum, Rosemary, plays golf at Faithlegg in east Waterford and she arranged a golf tournament and coffee morning which raised another €1,000 so I can't take any credit for that – thanks Mum!

A friend of mine has a restaurant in Waterford city centre so I contacted a musical friend of mine, a very talented lad called Tadhg Williams, and they both helped me to stage a themed night of song and food there. Tadhg was MC and we raised just over €1,000 from that night. I also did a bag pack at Tesco in Ardkeen and thanks to a few generous individuals I reached my fundraising goal, which was very satisfying personally. I met a lot of people back home during the year's fundraising (I'm based in Dublin) and getting to know fellow 'Pieta Challengers' on the weekend hikes on the Comeraghs re-connected me with Waterford. It also helped to build a real collegiate atmosphere among the group. Well in advance of boarding the plane to Addis Ababa, it really felt like we had each other's backs.

During the hikes, people who had really suffered, or who had experienced tragedy within their own families, opened up and shared their stories with those of us who have not been that soldier. It was humbling to reach such a level of acceptance with men and women who had been put through the wringer but here they were, still standing, freely sharing their experiences with us. They now wanted to reach out and make a difference in the lives of others who were still in the midst of their own difficulties. Lifelong friendships were made during that year of fundraising, hiking and story-telling, all thanks to one man's slightly crazy idea! At the outset of this endeavour, it had never occurred to me that I'd encounter this level of revelation and warmth, and I'm so, so pleased that I took a punt on what ultimately proved to be a life-altering, life-affirming experience.

The level of physical preparation for Kilimanjaro was unlike anything I'd been exposed to up to that juncture (having played soccer and rugby in school while dabbling in athletics), but I have to admit I found it all incredibly enjoyable. The knowledge transfer provided in the Comer-aghs by John Deegan, an avid hillwalker, was incredible. I got the feeling that John would be happiest were he cemented to a mountain given his enthusiasm levels and having only visited the Comeraghs on a handful of occasions prior to those sessions, I really gained a new-found appreciation for this natural treasure in the heart of County Waterford. Like Enda, John brought his skill, character and wit to bear throughout the training hikes, and he elevated and enriched the entire experience for me. A day in the hills with people of a similar mindset represents a day well spent. Work and personal foibles dissolved on the mountainside and, over those eight months, they grew so small as to become irrelevant. My thighs were strengthening and my eyes felt well and truly open. It was as good a feeling as I've ever known.

Prior to arriving in Tanzania, I hadn't spared too much thought to some of the less desirable scenarios that could unfold on the Kilimanjaro trail: be it nausea, altitude sickness, a bowel beyond irritability or a combination of all three and whatever else you're having. And in hindsight, I'm glad I didn't enter into all that much previsualisation. Out on the mountain, I was certainly among the luckier members of our group when it came to ailments. I might have been dehydrated on more than one occasion and had a few altitude-related headaches, but I never reached a point where any of those discomforts felt debilitating.

I kept going, which may well have been pot luck more than anything. When I saw how much altitude and Enda disagreed with each other, I felt incredibly bad for him because (a) I knew how hard he'd trained in advance of the trip and that his physical fitness greatly outweighed mine, and (b) this was his baby. We were all there because of his gentle powers of persuasion. The dice rolled kindly for me. My body reacted well to the thinning air while others with greater engines than mine really laboured in the altitude. Seeing people vomiting, even spasming, in the middle of the night when you're not entirely lucid yourself and watching on as some of the group were evacuated off the mountain due to illness were entirely unexpected experiences. This was alien territory for all of us, in terms of both mind and body, and there was no shame in feeling slightly scared at times. But there was also an incredible sense of solidarity throughout the trek. There may well have been a lot of discomfort within the group for considerable stages of the challenge, but nobody really vocalised that, which definitely helped the overall mood. We certainly shared the load of the washing machine along the ascent of Kilimanjaro but those aches and pains we could keep to ourselves remained within.

I know Enda wanted to be the one who unloaded the washing machine off his back on summit night. We all did. But even the best-laid plans don't always come to pass and ultimately his body told him what he couldn't do. The whole point of the challenge was about 'Sharing the Load' and ensuring that the washing machine got to the top of the mountain. After all, nobody can do everything entirely by themselves; everyone needs support at some stage in life and for me that was the pivotal message of the challenge. Enda is unquestionably a 'super man', but he's not the last son of Krypton - none of us are! If anything, the ultimate message emanating from Kilimanjaro became more symbolic when Enda, the leader of our gang, had to not only share the load but transfer it and entrust it to others. He had to reach out for help, and it was readily there for him.

Summit night was quite surreal. The final approach began at 1 a.m., so none of us had slept all that much in the hours beforehand. Stella Point is the peak before the peak, so to speak, and it's not all that far from the actual summit, a few hundred metres, but bridging that small stretch was no picnic. By the time I eventually reached the top, I was running on fumes. There I was, at one of the world's most spectacular locations, and I was too knackered to appreciate it. It was very cold up there - it wasn't the kind of temperature you'd be too comfortable hanging around in - and thoughts soon turned to what lay below the cloud line. We'd been on the mountain for seven days by then and we had all had our fill of it. I wish I could have appreciated the setting and the achievement more than I did, but I was too knackered and punch-drunk to truly take in the extent of the accomplishment there and then. But I'd done it. I could compute that much. I'd done it.

There was a really great dynamic within our group. There were a lot of nice people on the mountain who had rallied to Enda's cause and I think it's fair to say that we all made the most of it. At no stage did we lose sight of what had brought us out there: the decades-old failure of the State to adequately address the provision of mental health services with efforts such as the Pieta Challenge serving to highlight this massive social issue. Too many people have been let down by the State and this institutional inaction has spurred a lot of us 'ordinary' citizens into action.

And do you know what, if Enda comes calling again with another fundraising escapade in mind, I'd have no hesitation in signing up. Why not? I'm not sure what his next big plan is - there's got to be something brewing - but he'll know where to find me.

Leslie Hughes: Enda and Me

Summer 2016. I'd just left a job. I was also going through a rough patch, and I've known my share of them. I felt I needed a new hobby or a fresh outlet to latch onto in an attempt to get myself 'back to normal'. I realise there's probably a better way of putting it, but that's the only way I can describe my frame of mind right then. Things haven't always been straightforward for me – I've suffered from depression and anxiety for 25 years – and there are times when I can feel the fog approaching, when my whole world gets a great deal narrower and a lot more unsettled. And try as I did for those few weeks, nothing shifted my mindset into a higher gear. Instead, I reached a real low point. The fog grew thicker. Little did I think that a larger-than-life school teacher carrying a washing machine would metaphorically help to break my fall.

Kilimanjaro wasn't my first fundraising 'expedition'. In 2004, I spent three weeks in an orphanage in Moldova after responding to a call for volunteers from a big-hearted woman called Suzanne O'Connell. That trip was a complete eye-opener. To see children with a range of challenges and disabilities living in such difficult conditions was a game-changer. It made me want to do more to help other people facing a range of problems I had only experienced during nightmares. I was working in a call centre in Waterford at the time but when I got back from Moldova I knew I needed to change direction, so I kissed goodbye to that job. I had also crossed the Sinai Desert for Women's Aid, which was a big thing for me. And while I got a lot out of both of those trips, the biggest thing for me about both was that, in my own small way, I'd helped a few people. I'd also done some volunteering for ChildLine. I do think it's important to try to give something back. I like to help and, given my own background, helping like that has also helped me along the way. There have definitely been times when it's kept the fog at a safe distance.

When the Darkness into Light Walk was launched in Waterford, I signed up immediately. It's something my daughter Freya and I do together every year and to see thousands of yellow t-shirts moving along the Cork Road at four in the morning is just incredible. It shows how many individuals and families have been in the trenches, and as a three-time suicide survivor in my teens, I know what it's like to be down there, and not see any positive way out. Emotionally, things were pretty tough for me growing up. I struggled with my mental health from before my teens. There were other mental health issues in my home along with a very unhealthy relationship with alcohol. I was vulnerable and confused; unfortunately this made me easy prey. Just around my fifteenth birthday I was groomed, which led to abuse. What followed was years of self-medicating and not coping with my mental health. But for all the pain I've gone through, and this might sound perverse, part of me wouldn't change a thing because if I hadn't gone through all of that I don't think I'd have the openness and awareness I have now when it comes to talking about suicidal ideation, poor mental health, and wanting to help others.

Darkness into Light was also the first time I laid eyes on Enda O'Doherty and his washing machine. When I saw him strolling around with it on his back at the Regional Sports Centre, I thought he was cracked! I'd seen some of the videos he'd recorded during the Belfast to Waterford walk but didn't give too much thought to why he'd become so friendly with an appliance until I left that job in the summer of 2016, and read his Facebook post about his next Pieta Challenge: climbing Mount Kilimanjaro the following summer. Another fundraiser abroad felt like something which could help the fog to lift. It was an itch that needed to be scratched, giving me something to focus on at a time when my life needed a project. It also brought Enda into my life, and the lives of about 30 more of us who ended up on a plane with him bound for Ethiopia on the adventure of a lifetime. I contacted Enda on Facebook, and he rang me in double-quick time: Jesus, and I mean this in the best possible way, but he never shuts up! He gave me the spiel about Kilimanjaro, Pieta House, sharing the load, raising the €4,000 and, I swear to God, he did it all without even drawing a breath. And to think he made that speech to the 30 of us who ended up on the trip, and a few more who for their own reasons couldn't commit to it. He's a brilliant salesman and without doubt the most enthusiastic pain in the arse I've ever met! But you see, he's been down in the trenches too. He's worn that t-shirt. Enda O'Doherty is a good one. One of the best.

The fundraising side of things didn't feel like too daunting a task to commit to. Our intentions were genuine. Once I explained what I was doing and why I was doing it, people realised it wasn't about a free jolly in Africa and you wouldn't blame anyone for asking more than a few questions after all the bother with the likes of Console and so on. We were paying our way out there and raising money as well. There was no con involved in this whatsoever, and given the support Darkness into Light has received in Waterford and how well Pieta House has transmitted its message, it was fantastic to end up getting so much financial support. For a town which didn't do all that well during the Celtic Tiger years and is still taking its time to get back on its feet, there's great generosity in Waterford people. I ended up raising over €8,000, which would fund counselling for eight people for a year. That sum of money could potentially save eight lives and help eight families through such a traumatic period. When I went through my darkest times, I wish someone would have fought for me or that there would have been somewhere I could have gone to talk to someone. But there weren't many people talking about mental health in the 1990s: I had people telling me that I was just a drama queen and that I was faking things. That's just the way things were back then. But for people to able to open up now about suicide and depression (think about all those people we were told had 'the nerves' when we were growing up) is a huge step forward. That shift in public opinion feels like it's given me permission to talk about my own experiences. A lot of people hadn't heard about my story but in the spirit of the trip and its load-sharing mission statement, I made a video, posted it on my Facebook page and spoke about pretty much everything. And the freedom that I got from that was healing as well. Everything about this Enda-led adventure has been positive. It's been an incredible experience.

Landing at Addis Ababa was so, so exhilarating; I was child-like with excitement. The whole thing became utterly real when the African heat hit us on the apron of the airport. And once we caught sight of Kilimanjaro from the bus, it was a genuinely jaw-dropping moment. The ills at home were like pimples in comparison but nonetheless I just couldn't wait to get going the following morning.

With the exception of summit night, I'd been one of the luckier members of the party. And until things went completely pear-shaped at Stella Point, 600 feet from Uhuru Peak, Kilimanjaro hadn't been too hard on my body. I had music blaring on my phone during every leg of the journey and I was singing and dancing a good deal of the way up. I was eating and sleeping well, both of which were huge helps to me and I realised how lucky I was when I saw how tough some of the group were finding it on both those fronts. I was able to do a lot of things comfortably that people were struggling to do from quite an early stage in the trek (and I'm hardly the sportiest), and while I wouldn't say that made me feel bullet-proof, I was in a position to enjoy the experience a good deal more than most, until the last night that is, just 170 metres from the official finish line, with Africa's top floor in sight.

The final push for the summit began at 1 a.m. The dead of night. Seven hours into that walk and with Stella Point still an hour away, my head began to hurt. My guide, Emmanuel, immediately identified my difficulty and he couldn't have been better, checking my food and fluid intake. I had to sit down and ingest a few glucose tablets. It was freezing cold, it was dark and James Whelan, one of our travelling party who'd also been doing well up to that point, looked at me and I looked at him. He later told me that at that moment, as we shared a glance, he thought he was going to die. By then, things were getting slightly surreal for me; it felt as if I was in a dream. But Emmanuel got me gently back onto my feet and we got moving again, albeit gingerly, but within a matter of minutes, I began to fade in and out. Everything went dark. I could hear Emmanuel saying: 'I see you, I see you', and when I opened my eyes again, feeling like I was back in semi-reality, everything around me was white and gold. I had to sit down again and I ended up alongside John Deegan, the man who had brilliantly guided and trained us in the Comeragh Mountains for the previous few months, but he appeared to be completely golden to me at that disorientated moment. He was like a statue, while everything around him was white. I remember looking at him and then, like someone flicking a switch, I was gone.

I don't remember all that much thereafter. I can recall a lot of different voices and the odd glimpse of the doctor treating me but apparently I collapsed and then started shaking. Daire Grant, a good friend of Enda's, who is also a member of the Waterford Fire Service, came over to me and couldn't have been better. 'Come on Leslie', he said, which I can just about remember. 'Think about Jason [my husband]; think about the kids', and then the doctor came along. He attempted to put a line into me to get a drip running, and Daire cut my coat off to help the doctor do his job. I would later discover that I stopped breathing on two occasions during my episode. I have epilepsy but I hadn't had a seizure in the previous twelve years; I knew that you could stop breathing during an episode. It subsequently transpired that I hadn't had an epileptic seizure: my brain had swollen due to a different form of altitude sickness. Had I walked beyond Stella Point, I could have been in huge trouble as my brain needed more oxygen by then. The outcome could have been entirely different.

While I was evacuated, my eyes were opening and closing and I was passing in and out. It was a very odd feeling as I still have a lot of blanks about what exactly was happening to me and what people were doing to help me, and it really wasn't until I was almost off the mountain that I fully regained consciousness. I was taken down a dusty, steep route which is considered a shortcut. Two guides physically took me down, securing an arm each, while another walked behind me holding the drip and a fourth carried my gear. Daire wanted to come with me but I told him to go ahead, given that we were at Stella Point and so close to the peak, so he reluctantly agreed to do that, leaving the guides to get me down to thicker air. They were incredible, feeding me with sweet tea as I continued to speak complete gibberish, while my legs bobbed beneath me like linen on a clothes line. We reached the base of the mountain, I was administered oxygen and everything, in general, was okay. I was absolutely shattered but grateful to be still in one piece, even though I was somewhat 'out of it' for the following 24 hours. And to see everyone else back off the mountain, given how ill a few of us had been, was an enormous relief. I'd reached Stella Point and that was good enough for me. I wasn't disappointed in any way about not getting to the ultimate peak. The only thing that did bother me was I never got to leave a memento for my husband's cousin, Nicola Behan, who had died by suicide three years previously, under a rock at Uhuru. I did leave a picture and some of the green ribbon I'd brought in her memory under a tower of stones at Machame Camp. I'll leave the rest of the ribbon for Nicola somewhere else on another trek.

Were Enda to take on another adventure, sure it would certainly give me some food for thought alright. By the time we were all safely off Kilimanjaro and of slightly sounder minds and bodies, the catch-call was: 'What's the next challenge?' But once the adrenaline – and medication in some cases – had worn off, it hit me how time-consuming taking on a physical challenge like that had proven. The previous 12 months leading up to Kilimanjaro had just been swallowed up by it – you're living and breathing it and it's like any busy spell in your life – you don't realise just how much you were doing or how you kept doing it until you click the pause button. The Pieta Challenge became a live-in partner for a year so if something was to present itself a few years from now, I think I'd be good to go again alright. The rest of Nicola's green ribbon is still at home and

I'd like to leave that on top of another mountain, perhaps. Another itch of mine might well need scratching soon enough.

I'll conclude by sharing a memory of Enda O'Doherty that will never, ever leave me. It was during one of our early training treks up the Comeraghs and he was walking in front of me, carrying a bag full of rocks on his back, as Enda tends to do. We're chatting away - sure he's so easy to talk to - and then he began to feel a bit ill. I suggested he should take a few rocks out of the bag but he was politely having none of it. 'No', Enda told me, as his face grew greener. 'I have to keep pushing, must keep pushing', and then his heavy breathing began to kick in. 'Jesus', I said to him with a grin, 'it's like walking alongside a porn star with all the grunting you're doing!' Within seconds, Enda began to dry-retch, and I jumped over the biggest rock I could find, and our mountain coach, John Deegan, was screaming at me: 'Don't walk on rocks, don't veer off.' By then, Enda was getting sick - the wind was blowing, and carrying the vomit with it. Luckily, I'd avoided the blast radius. When we stopped a few minutes later, and after John had given me a bit of a dressing-down (in fairness, he was only doing his job), I said to Enda, 'I love you like a brother but I don't love you enough to stand in the line of fire and get puked on!'

But I really do love Enda like a brother. And yes, there are times when he can be like an annoying brother, and I tell him that too. He's a force of nature; he gets ideas and runs with them. He has an addictive personality, which is something I share in common with him and that's probably one of the reasons why we get on so well. I've fed off his energy and he has helped to light a spark in me. What else can I say? He's just an amazing man and I'm all the better a person for knowing him.

Sharing the Festive Load

'Dig deep within yourself, for there is a fountain of goodness ever ready to flow if you will keep digging.'

Marcus Aurelius

Christmas is a time of conflicting emotions. While we can bask in the afterglow of children's laughter as they busily undo that wrapping paper you meticulously concealed a present in, those quieter, reflective moments, maybe standing at a loved one's grave, give us reason to pause. To draw breath. To take stock. It's a time of year when an over-riding sense of loss can, in so many cases, outweigh the cork-popping joy the advertising world otherwise directs us to feel each Christmas morning.

The 'busy-ness' of life can be overwhelming, particularly at Christmastime when you consider the self-inflicted demands we make on our time: be it shopping, the work night out, the trip to the panto, cooking or hosting the relatives we mightn't have the greatest of relationships with. We all know the drill. Of course, life itself, from one end of the year to the other, can be overwhelming; the points raised here are not exclusively reserved for that final week on the calendar. But, for many, the Christmas/New Year holiday can prove a time of polarising sentiment: gratitude for what we have and grief for what we've lost.

Yet the good news is that there's more help out there than ever before, at the opposite end of a phone line, through an email or even face to face, in a quiet, non-judgemental atmosphere. And that help can make today a little more bearable than yesterday and bring the dawn a little closer. The fact that there's no one in Ireland today living more than 50 miles away from a Pieta House demonstrates a visible public commitment to supporting those who feel emotionally and mentally listless.

The message I've been committed to for the better part of four years, through the washing machine adventures between Belfast and Waterford and taking it up Mount Kilimanjaro, has been all about 'Sharing the Load' and asking for help. And if you want to Share the Load, you can call Pieta on 1800-247-247 or other services including Teac Tom in Kilkenny or the Samaritans to name but three.

When we say 'Happy Christmas', it's fair to say that we mean those words and that we want Christmas to be an enjoyable time for as many people as possible, but I think a lot of people find Christmas very tough. It's a time when a lot of us remember family and friends we may have lost through illness or suicide.

Christmas provides the perfect storm for negative mental health. You probably end up spending too much money, and even when you've spent that money, you probably feel guilty that you didn't spend more, or you wish you had more to spend on your family, all of which leads to financial pressure for a hardly insignificant number of people. The Christmas holidays come along and you might end up staying up the first night and watching a box set, and then you might do the same thing the next night, and you find yourself staying up later and inevitably getting up later the following morning and your whole sleep pattern out of kilter.

And when you factor in the additional time spent with family, and the additional amounts of food we traditionally shovel into ourselves each Christmas, stress levels can rise. If you eat rubbish, you'll feel rubbish and let's face it, Christmas for a lot of us is about turkey sandwiches, a few Quality Street on the side and other crazy food combinations. It's more grazing than eating. And then you throw in all those aforementioned factors and you're reminded of the season's abnormality. And of course, being Ireland, there's alcohol to throw into the mix as well, and drinking a lot is not going to solve your problems: if anything, it's going to magnify that sense of loss and emptiness.

So if you tend to find Christmas a struggle, make a conscious effort to be kind to yourself. Try to keep some level of routine. Definitely celebrate: we all need that extra spoon of trifle after a long year but you have to take the time to invest in yourself, to invest in your mental health, and if you are having a tough time then reach out, Share the Load and ask for help. There are so many good people out there who want to help you. In my experience, a problem shared really is a problem halved. And once you opt for such a path, life can and will improve.

You can call Pieta House on 1800-247-247,
Teac Tom on 056-7796592 or
the Samaritans on 116-123.

Endnotes

1   *Wooden: A Lifetime of Observations and Reflections on and off the Court*, Coach John Wooden with Steve Jamison (New York, NY: McGraw-Hill, 1997).

2   *The Big Fellow: Michael Collins and the Irish Revolution*, Frank O'Connor (Nashville, TN: Thomas Nelson and Sons, 1937).

3   *How Champions Think: In Sports and in Life*, Dr Bob Rotella with Bob Cullen (New York, NY: Simon & Schuster, 2015).

4   'Family Mourns "Surreal" Death of Woman on Mount Kilimanjaro,' *Irish Times*, Olivia Kelleher, 27 July 2017.

5   *The West Wing*, Season 1, Episode 13, created by Aaron Sorkin (NBC Television, 1999–2006).

6   *Until Victory Always - A Memoir*, Jim McGuinness with Keith Duggan (Dublin: Gill Books, 2015).

7   *How Champions Think*, Dr Bob Rotella with Bob Cullen.

8   *How Champions Think*, Dr Bob Rotella with Bob Cullen.

9   *Wooden*, Coach John Wooden with Steve Jamison.

10 *Wooden*, Coach John Wooden with Steve Jamison.

11 'For in the final analysis ...' - a speech by President John Fitzgerald Kennedy, American University, Washington DC, 10 June 1963.

12 *Wooden*, Coach John Wooden with Steve Jamison.

13 *Ernest Hemingway on Writing*, Larry W Philips (London: Scriber, 2002).

14 *The Pressure Principle: Handle Stress, Harness Energy and Perform When It Counts*, Dr Dave Alred MBE (London: Penguin Life, 2016).

15 *The Pressure Principle*, Dr Dave Alred MBE.

16 'Incomparable Grief as Elisha Laid to Rest,' *Munster Express*, Dermot Keyes, 6 April 2018.

Bibliography

Alred, Dr Dave (2016), *The Pressure Principle: Handle Stress, Harness Energy and Perform When It Counts*, London: Penguin Life.

Holiday, Ryan and Hanselman, Stephen (2016), *The Daily Stoic: 366 Meditations on Wisdom, Perseverance and the Art of Living*, London: Profile Books.

Kelleher, Olivia, 'Family Mourns "Surreal" Death of Woman on Mount Kilimanjaro', *Irish Times*, 27 July 2017.

Keyes, Dermot, 'Incomparable Grief as Elisha Laid to Rest', *Munster Express*, 6 April 2018.

McGuinness, Jim with Duggan, Keith (2015), *Until Victory Always - A Memoir*, Dublin: Gill Books.

O'Connor, Frank (1937), *The Big Fellow: Michael Collins and the Irish Revolution*, Nashville, TN: Thomas Nelson and Sons.

Philips, Larry W. (2002), *Ernest Hemingway on Writing*, London: Scriber.

Rotella, Dr Bob with Cullen, Bob (2015), *How Champions Think: In Sports and in Life*, New York, NY: Simon & Schuster.

Serena, Katie, 'Peter Freuchen: The Real Most Interesting Man in the World', https://allthatsinteresting.com/peter-freuchen, 15 November 2017.

Wooden, John with Jamison, Steve (1997), *Wooden: A Lifetime of Observations and Reflections on and off the Court*, New York, NY: McGraw-Hill.

'For in the final analysis...' A speech by President John Fitzgerald Kennedy, American University, Washington DC, 10 June 1963.

Hamlet, William Shakespeare.

Meditations, Marcus Aurelius.

The Empire Strikes Back, Lucasfilm, 1980.

The West Wing, Aaron Sorkin, NBC Television, 1999–2006.